Say Good Night

**By
Richard Burns**

Damnation Books, LLC.
P.O. Box 3931
Santa Rosa, CA 95402-9998
www.damnationbooks.com

Say Good Night
by Richard Burns

Digital ISBN: 978-1-61572-620-2
Print ISBN: 978-1-61572-621-9

Cover art by: Dawné Dominique
Edited by: Kim Richards

Copyright 2012 author

Printed in the United States of America
Worldwide Electronic & Digital Rights
1st North American, Australian and UK Print Rights

All rights reserved. No part of this book may be
reproduced, scanned or distributed in any form,
including digital and electronic or mechanical,
including photocopying, recording, or by any
information storage and retrieval system, without
the prior written consent of the Publisher, except for
brief quotes for use in reviews.

This book is a work of fiction. Characters, names,
places and incidents either are the product of the
author's imagination or are used fictitiously, and any
resemblance to any actual persons, living or dead,
events, or locales is entirely coincidental.

To the ones who couldn't make it home, no matter how hard they tried, they just couldn't get there.

To Kathie, for Being my wife. To my cousin Nancy for coming to visit.

To the men who served with me from 1979-2010. I'm a better man today, just for knowing you!

Chapter One

Week ending 7/25/09
Bagram Airfield, Bagram, Afghanistan, Friday, 23:00

I finally arrived at the beach paradise of Bagram, Afghanistan. It was the only beach paradise with no water or women, to speak of. None for me anyways. Unfortunately, it was far too late to try to locate my youngest brother, Martin who was just about to finish his first tour with almost a year in country now.

For anybody who has never been here before, the difference since my last 'vacation' is startling. Bagram, is the name of the tiny village on the floor of a valley surrounded by high ridges of mountains on all sides. Many of the tops have snow well into May. This flat piece of ground was the selected sight for the Russian Army and Air Force to build their largest Airfield, once upon a time. After a fair amount of decay, the once derelict, abandoned Russian Airfield is now a bustling and booming metropolis. Complete with Pizza Hut, Burger King and Dairy Queen. These were all on the American airfield, naturally. The population of the Firebase had grown from an estimated 5,000 at any given time due to units in transition, to close to 50,000. Not all of them American. The Polish presence has come on in a big way, as well as the French and Italians. With them, comes a certain level of creature comforts. I can't say that I was entirely disappointed with that. As late as it was now however, those could wait.

As for my brother Martin, he was just decorated for heroism in the face of the enemy. Courage under fire is no small thing to me. Having been there myself a few times, I happen to know just how hard it is to keep your wits about you, much less perform with valor and distinction. This, in his very first action, no less. Such courage on your initial encounter with the enemy is very rare. Even more elusive is the chance that somebody else sees it, and recognizes it as a courageous act, and then goes to the trouble of writing you up for it and submitting it for decoration.

In June, his platoon was ambushed while running in convoy back to his Forward Operating Base at Gardez, when Soviet Anti-Tank Rockets went streaking through the night leaving trails of sparks and smoke in their wakes. These Rocket Propelled Grenades RPG's were hurling themselves toward the convoy's vehicles, with one passing just in front of his vehicle. The Platoon did as they had rehearsed a hundred times and high-tailed it out of the kill zone just as fast as their engines could carry them. This is actually fairly typical. Mission #1: clear the kill zone! Do whatever is necessary to get yourself off of the X. Small arms fire raked over the convoy, searching for any exposed bodies, green tracers swept up and down the column of vehicles from a dozen different points.

As the enemy fire raked up and down the convoy, Martin's Platoon Sergeant who was traveling at the rear of the convoy, managed to catch up to Martin's vehicle and flag him to a stop, inside the kill zone. He informed Martin of a vehicle which had taken a hit and was now stopped in the middle of the not-so-sweet spot. They still had two wounded men back there, so without a second's thought, Martin and his Platoon Sergeant swung their vehicles back around and went back, further into the Kill zone to rescue their comrades.

When they got to the vehicles, they pulled their armored Hummers into a position that would allow them some cover and a 'safe' place to work all things being relative. While under continuous enemy fire, the two wounded men were removed from the crippled vehicle and Martin with his platoon Sergeant, treated their wounds and prepared the men for removal. One man required a stretcher though and therefore, could not be removed in a Hummer. An MRAP *Mine Resistant Armored Personnel Carrier: these are much longer and taller armored vehicles designed to carry an eleven man Rifle squad with much thicker armor than even on an armored Hummer*, was brought back into the Kill zone so that the stretcher case could be laid flat upon the floor.

No such luck. The Stretcher was too long, so the wounded soldier had to be laid upon the roof of one Hummer and Martin remained on the hood of the vehicle, completely exposed to the enemy's fire, holding the wounded soldier's IV bag on one hand with his M-4 carbine in the other to provide covering fire, as they drove out of the kill zone. Riding out of the kill zone, sitting on the hood of a vehicle, Martin must've surely felt like the worm on the end of a hook. I couldn't wait to see him again, because it's a beautiful thing when Heroism's highest honor is bestowed upon a brave man. That honor being the right to walk around in your own skin for another day.

Say Good Night

Now, it was my day in the barrel.

Bagram. The last time I saw it was in my rearview mirror, where it should be and it never looked better. Bagram has changed so much since my last vacation, I don't want to try to find Martin at this hour. Furthermore, apparently they have expanded several new, let's call them "housing developments" to include a tent city, several miles away, where Martin's "condo" is located. First thing in the morning will have to do.

* * * *

Saturday, 08:00
Well, I had to take a bus, a subway and six miles on camel back, cross eight rivers, two streams and a gorge, but I found him. He was sleeping like the lazy bum that he is! Actually, he was sleeping the Brave Man's Sleep. He woke easily enough and it good to see him.

He filled me in on all of the details of his exploits and adventures. Unfortunately, Saturday was the only day we had together. I had to be on duty Sunday, and he had to go to lock down at the Airfield in order to fly home the next day.

For those of you who might be wondering, there is no competition between Martin and I for medals. I'm quite happy and proud to let him be the hero of the family. While I'm sure all of us were somewhat surprised, initially. However, I think that we all knew that he was always made of the stuff of heroes. The only surprise was that it was finally recognized. None of us were really all that shocked. After all, he comes from hearty stock! Me? I still plan to hang my decorations when I retire. It's also my plan that there be *no* Purple Hearts among them!

Now, for the good stuff...

* * * *

Monday, 11:00
It was another glorious day in Afghanistan. This is the same as to say that it sucked. I frequently get the question, "So, what was it like over there?"

To these people I typically reply, "Do you know that feeling that you get in the summer, when you go to the beach and you first step into the hot blistering sand for the first time?"

When the individual shakes his head 'yes', I'll follow through with, "It feels just like that, except over your entire body and it lasts for a year."

112 degrees Fahrenheit in the shade. There is no shade. The scorpion on the sand bag next to me held my amusement for a minute, but only until he discovered my presence. I drew the knife that my father gave me prior to my first tour in '03, and used it to pin him to the sandbag. He continued to twitch and sting the blade of my knife in his death throes. I thought to myself, *a Tasmanian Wide tail, allegedly the most deadly of all scorpions.* I never believe such things. Watching his last twitches, *Sucks to be you'* I thought to myself.

Well, truth be told, today isn't the best day to be me, either. I took a moment to look over the vast expanse that was my kingdom. At least for the time being. No matter, tonight, I had an appointment.

Tommy approached and said, "We have a meet tonight. With "Bijoux." That same source you met the other night. He says he wants to talk to you, though. Hurts my feelings, a little". Tommy was in country for a month by the time I arrived, so he was trying to point out that he had been working for the last four weeks while I was home on leave. He's such a bastard!

Actually, Tommy Allen was slightly older than me approaching fifty at the time, rather small framed wiry man with balding sandy brown hair and a fantastic sense of humor. I say wiry and small framed, he was a very 'plain' looking sort of man. Very unsuspecting. In fact, he was the perfect, "Gray Man". The one who nobody remembers, if that's the way he wants it. He was, like me, another Michigander.

22:00

Tommy and I were at the front gate to the firebase that leads into the booming sprawling Central Asian slum that is Bagram. Our Lieutenant asked us the preliminary questions.

"Tommy, your code name is…?"

"Angry Hardcore."

"Kind of long for a code name isn't it?"

"It's a very long story and it involves an Irishman by the name of Bailey, also known as the Angry Muffin. Don't make me give any details."

"The memory is too painful for Tommy," I said.

"The Angry Muffin? Angry Hardcore? You guys are awfully angry," the Lieutenant said.

"You have no idea," I said.

Tommy got serious for a moment, counted out the characters on his fingers to get to the required number six, "Let's go with that one, call me Bailey," Tommy said at last.

"Rick, your code name?" he asked of me.

"I'm the arbiter of death, the reaper of the Taliban, the bringer of doom. Mine is the name which strikes fear into the hearts of men. That makes the most brutal tremble at its mention. I am...'Binkey'."

"Good one."

"And you guys are going to meet with...?"

"Bijoux."

"ID cards...? I'll leave them with the gate guard with instructions to call you in missing if you aren't back inside the wire by 01:00."

With that, Tommy and I slipped outside the wire. Our meeting would normally have been a ten minute walk from the front gate, but we had to take a rather round-about course to make sure we hadn't picked up a tail and then reconnoiter around the meet site, then establish some surveillance. I wanted to get there early to leave Tommy in an over watch position where he could give me covering fire the meeting turned to shit. Somebody to watch for any movement around our meet sight, to see if Bijoux had brought friends in the hopes of taking me, or if he were unknowingly followed.

We always have a kill signal because we almost never have practical radio communication. With Tommy, if I'd been in overwatch while he made the approach and he found that the situation was rotten, either it wasn't Bijoux, or it was and he was followed, or if we'd been betrayed in any way, I'd have him, Bijoux in my cross hairs the entire time he met with Tommy. Then, if and when Tommy gave his kill signal, I'd have squeezed the trigger, sending him to an alternate plane of existence. With Tommy, who is a non-smoker, his kill signal would be to pull out a cigarette and as soon as he struck the lighter, Bijoux would cease to be.

However, Bijoux wanted to speak to me specifically. My guess is Tommy, just didn't gel with him. Who knows?

* * * *

22:45
I moved up to my far recognition point, behind the shell station, and waited for my "appointment" to arrive. I stood in the

dark, wearing a native scarf and head cover, to make my silhouette look more natural with my surroundings. I waited another thirty minutes before I saw Bijoux's signal. He flicked his lighter as though he were trying to light a cigarette. Five flicks. Had he actually lit his cigarette, it would've meant that he was followed, the meeting was off and Tommy would've moved into action. Because it destroys your night vision, naturally, it's not a good idea to use matches or lights for signaling at night, but nobody had enough time to work out a better signal.

I moved forward and gave my near recognition, *"Fuer?"*

He stepped forward and I struck the lighter lighting his cigarette and making sure the face was his. It was.

"They have something big planned. Bigger than you or I ever dreamed of."

"How about a few specifics?"

"I don't know. I think it involves some genius-ly forged documents. They tell me they have sources inside of your White House! It will break everything! Your coalition against us; your relations with the Chinese; your relations with Canada...the English. *Everything!*" He said this all in frantic whispers.

"What makes you say that?" I that instant a single gunshot rang out just about fifty yards away, Bijoux arched his back and collapsed. He was dead before his last breath left his mouth.

I drew my Beretta and scanned the area. *There!* Across what passed for a road on the other block behind the Junk shop, a shadow in a man-dress Haji garb was trying to level an additional shot at me. This is something I always take very personal. He fires as I step into a doorway. I hear the bullet crack as it passes by. I can see the muzzle spit a small flash the very same instant that I squeeze off my shot. *Lousy motherfucker!* I fired once, and the shadow was gone. I ran around to the front of the gas station to try for another shot as he came out on the street side, but he never emerges. He must've run parallel to the shops there, or I got him.

Tommy came walking down to me, his pistol drawn. I ask, "Hey, Tommy. Where were you?"

"I can tell you where I wasn't. I wasn't anywhere around here."

"What were you doing?"

"Not worrying about you."

"Thanks."

"Hell, you've hit everybody you've ever shot at. Why would I worry?" he said giving me his best Alfred E. Newman smile.

We approach the Junk shop and I came around the front, while

Tommy came around the back through a parallel side 'street'.

We both met up where I had seen the shooter. Tommy feeling his oats, quipped, "Looks like you've broken your streak. Ha! You missed!"

I flashed my pen light down into the pool of blood that was already starting to congeal in the sand. I simply said back, "No, I didn't. I got him." We both began to follow the blood trail, down the street, and around a corner, when about 200 yards in front us, a car suddenly started and pulled away from the curb at a high rate of speed.

"There he goes," I said.

"Yep." With street lights still decades away, we could get no description of the vehicle, much less a plate. Not that a plate number would matter. I knew there wasn't a national database of vehicle registrations. So, with this failure, we returned to base.

* * * *

09:00, The following Morning

The Combined Joint Special Operations Task Force-Afghanistan CJSOTF-A, pronounced, See Juh Soh Tuf, runs a twenty-four hour Joint Operations Center, or JOC pounced, Jock, which tracks every unit deployed and follows them through their operations and all enemy contacts.

However, since Intelligence Operations tend to be substantially more sensitive and often classified at levels beyond those of the average Special Forces Operator, the Intelligence Directorate established a separate Operations Center to track Intelligence teams and Operators on the ground. This is called the Joint Intelligence Operations Center, and since there is no cool word that can be made from that acronym, we simply call it the OPCEN.

As we came into the CJSOTF headquarters, we both checked our distribution boxes and began looking over the latest Intelligence Analysis Summary, this is called an INTSUM in 'the business'.

A small parade from British Intelligence passed us and filed into the conference room behind us. The last in the procession was a striking, *very shapely* brunette with what I call 'subtle beauty'. Her beauty was not overpowering, but always clearly present and everybody was always aware of it. Of course, she was always aware that everybody else was aware. Every man was always looking for the non-existent panty lines, or trying to get a glimpse down the front of her blouse. She knew this too and often gave her hips a very saucy, sometimes blatant sway. It depended on who was watching. I noticed that she did this every single time I was around. Not altogether sure it was for my benefit, though.

Since she is a valued colleague, I should take a second to introduce her. I don't know why she took the sort of friendship with me that she did in such a short time. I had walked in on a conversations that she was having with a couple of other women about her wedding dress, obviously she was married I now knew.

I made one simple off-color joke, "So? You decided to wear white anyways?" This brought me clear into the center of Moneypenny's radar screen.

She was an intelligence analyst from MI-6 Britain's equivalent of the CIA, and she reminded me so much of another character of Ian Flemming's, *James Bond* series. Her name was Barbara Frost, and I thought the name Barbara so drab for such a beauty. So naturally, I took the liberty to draw the parallel to James Bond's 'Moneypenny'. I think she stepped into the roll admirably. Once she knew she caught my eye, the saucy sway began. *So, it is for my benefit...*

Moneypenny was very smart, very sexy and extremely desirable. However, being a beautiful woman working in a Man's world, such as the British Ministry of Defense MOD, is tough. She was a woman who wanted to be a woman. Who wanted to be sexy, desirable and beautiful, but at the same time, she wanted to be taken seriously, treated professionally. Yet at the very same time, treated like the beautiful woman she is. Apparently, she likes to push the envelope, so to speak, regarding her undeniable sexiness. You'll see why I say 'apparently' in just a second.

"Good morning, Moneypenny. How are you?" I asked.

In her most pleasant accent, and in a very seductive tone of voice, she laid a hand on my forearm, the same in which hand I held the INTSUM I was reading, and she said "Completely shaven."

As she said this, my eyes came up from the paper that was no longer of interest to me and I looked at the far wall. Then, as though my head were on a swivel, I turned to look her in those gorgeous blue eyes as she smiled at me so brightly, then let go of my arm and stepped inside the conference room.

"What did you say?" I asked, still not believing that I could possibly have heard her correctly.

She just smiled and gave me a sort 'toodaloo' wave of her

fingers. She closed the door, and was out of sight. The sign on the door said, 'Meeting in progress. No interruptions'.

"Tommy! Did you hear what she just said?"

"What who said?" He looked up annoyed because I had distracted him.

"Never mind," I said.

"Come on, we've got some 'splaining to do," doing a lame Ricky Ricardo impersonation.

"What's this 'we' shit white man!? I was doing what I was supposed to be doing! You were the one who was out to lunch."

"Hey, I didn't shoot anybody," Tommy protested.

"That's the problem, you lazy bum." I thought to myself, *Sucks to be me.*

Chapter Two

Week ending 7/31/09
Sunday, 07:00

Tommy and I wandered around the streets of Kabul in search of our assassin, figuring he would need medical attention, and would not want to wait too long to get it. He would not go to any possible facilities in Bagram, and given that Kabul in only an hour away, well... That's where we were now, with the only cab driver who spoke an acceptable level of English, and claimed to know all of the hospitals and medical clinics in Kabul.

What a garden spot Kabul is! The streets of Kabul are a maze of adobe shacks and a hundred larger adobe compounds called qallats. Most of the Coalition Forces call them 'Mud Huts'. Except for the major highways and recently constructed developments, the streets of Kabul don't appear to run in anything resembling a straight line. In most, if not all of the poor class neighborhoods where ever there was once a clear spot that could've served as a road or a street, somebody built a shack there, and then another, and another, *ad infinitum*. Neither Tommy, nor I were anywhere near savvy enough to take on the task.

* * * *

13:00
We had our guy. He was lying in a bed, with a bullet wound to his lower right abdomen, and had staggered in for treatment at around 01:30, claiming he was shot by an American at an Afghan National Army, Traffic Control Point TCP. Tommy went to check to see if any of our TCP's reported any shots fired last night, and none were had. Without ever looking at him, or letting him see our faces, we had him transferred to the hospital at Bagram Airfield BAF, and escorted by the Afghan National Police, while we followed the ambulance at a safe comfortable distance.

* * * *

16:00

Now within the safe and friendly confines of BAF, he was in the hospital under guard by American Military Police. He was not officially being detained because once he is, officially, we have only ninety-six hours from that minute to charge him as an Unlawful Enemy Combatant and make the case for further extended detention, or kick him loose. Therefore, we had a U.S. Army Special Forces Medic from the Combined Joint Special Operations Task Force—Afghanistan, dressed as a Doctor, change his bandages twice a day and try to chat him up. The excuse for his presence in the American hospital was explained as Kabul Doctor's concern for infection and our access to better antibiotics.

In reality, we were going to let him stew in his own juices for about two days, before we began our interrogation of him.

* * * *

Tuesday, 13:00

"I swear, I must've caught the incurable crud from that cab on Sunday. Ever since we got back, I have this rash that has been climbing up my back towards my shoulders," Tommy complained as we walked into the coffee room at the Joint Intelligence Operations Center.

"You whiney little bitch," I said as I leaned back against the counter with my coffee.

"No, I'm serious. Here. Look," he said as he stripped off his shirt.

Moneypenny walked in as he was pulling his shirt up over his head, I said simply "Moneypenny." She smiled at me, acknowledging my greeting—*an unusually tepid greeting from her, this is curious*—and without a word, stood beside me and commenced to making herself a cup of tea.

Tommy now had his shirt off and his back to me with his arm crooked behind him trying to point at this large red patch of what looked to me like, prickly heat.

"Does it itch?" I asked Tommy.

At this question, Moneypenny sprang into life. She swung her head to face me, and put her hand on my forearm again, and said, "Oh, no. It doesn't itch at all. I've been shaving since I was fifteen years old, and the secret is to use lots and lots of moisturizing oils and lotions. I take handfuls of oil, everyday and I just rub it into my skin there, so much oil that it's just flowing over my fingers.

Three, four, maybe five or six times a day."

I was vaguely aware of Tommy's simultaneous response, "No, it really just burns."

Once again, Moneypenny had my full attention. With the sort of self control that can move mountains, I looked at her with my best deadpan expression and said, "Thank you Moneypenny. I was quite worried."

"Hey Rick! My back...?" Tommy cried piteously.

She smiled a very sinister grin, "I knew you would be."

"After all, razor burn can be so...discomforting," I replied.

"Not to worry. I'm as *moist*, soft and smooth as a rose petal. Albeit, a very *hot* rose petal."

In this exact same moment, Brigadier George Ferguson walked into the break room to look at Tommy, stooped forward at the waist, shirt off arm crooked behind his back, brandishing that fish-belly white complexion of his, arm and elbow crooked at odd angles. It was all so perfect.

The Brigadier waved Tommy's report of the other night's events in his face and asked, "Just what were you doing while Burns was meeting with the source?"

"I was in the overwatch position, Sir." Tommy said as he straightened and replaced his shirt.

Moneypenny went on, "In fact, I think now is a good time to moisturize." With that, she picked up her tea and made for the door. Once she was behind the Brigadier, she stopped, turned and gave me another smile and a toodaloo wave of her fingers. Then, she was gone. It would be pointless to ask Tommy if he had heard the conversation, mired in his own problems. Right now, with the Brigadier in his face, those problems were considerable.

"You did *what*, precisely, when this gunman decided to terminate your source?"

"Well, when I first saw the man, I knew he was out of pistol range, which is all I had. In the next second, he fired and it was too late to do anything."

"So, essentially you're telling me you did nothing. Do I understand that correctly? That's shoddy work, Tommy," Ferguson said.

"How come he's Tommy and I'm just Burns?" I asked, feeling a little slighted not being on a first name basis with the Brigadier.

"Don't worry, Mister Burns. If he keeps this shyte up, his name will be Mudd," Ferguson said to me. However, I took a few moments to revel in Tommy's current...discomfort.

Say Good Night

* * * *

14:00

We had the MPs bring our "patient" to the Bagram Detention Facility, since we already knew that he could be moved. We wanted him to have a couple of days to fatten up, get a taste of relative luxury, all the while his fears and apprehensions eating away at him. The Detention Facility was an administrative office complex at one time for some bureaucracy, was three stories high with the first floor virtually one large open room. Into which we, the U.S. Forces threw and stacked and endless maze of steel wire cages, then put up a high block wall around the entire structure.

Tommy and I had decided on a strategy that we thought might work and work quickly with this guy. However, not having met him before, we were just shooting from the hip. Both of us in civilian clothes, we walked into one of the interrogation rooms at the detention facility.

"Mister Abu Said Lamas? I'm Colonel Binkus, and this is Major Eyemuhbad Sunovabytchz of the Russian FSB. Are you familiar with them? The Russian Federal Security Bureau?" I said it all so casually, as though it were idle chit-chat, but very much intended to push him off balance and rattle his cage a little. I continued, "They replaced the old KGB," I pointed at Tommy who was going to be virtually silent during this initial interview, primarily because he doesn't speak any Russian, and because I wanted to use his presence as an unforeseen sledgehammer. As long as he stood there, silent and indifferent to his existence, he remained the sword of Damocles, hanging over Abu's head.

He smiled up at me when I introduced myself, but it was the sort of smile that said, *"I'm getting over on you! I know a secret,"* and then when I mentioned a potential Russian in the equation, his smile went from sugar to shit in a second flat. *Bingo!* I thought to myself. Technically, it's against regulations to impersonate a senior rank, especially a very senior officer, without prior approval, and it's certainly against regulations to impersonate an officer of an allied nation. However, I wanted to stroke this guy's ego and terrify him at the same time. Keep him off balance. In addition, since we were acting under the authority and direction of a Brigadier, who out-ranks a Colonel, there was really very little difference. It's a fine point.

I received such a positive response upon mentioning the KGB, I decided to keep beating that drum. I followed through with another punch, "In fact, weren't you one of those old timers,

Eyemuhbad?" The first part I directed to our new friend Abu, and the second half I said turning to Tommy. Tommy nodded and gave a good guttural groan to pass for a 'yes'.

"Abu we understand that you say you were shot by an American soldier at a Control Point. The problem here is, that none of our CP's reported shooting anybody last night."

"They are lying," he said. He was trying to sound angry and indignant. However, his voice cracked at almost every third word, a sure sign he was more scared than mad.

"Now you see Abu, herein lays the problem. A local citizen was murdered last night after one of our MPs lit his cigarette for him. Now that MP said he shot the suspect with a 9mm pistol, just like this bullet that was pulled from you at the hospital in Kabul," I said holding up a nearly pristine 9mm bullet that I recovered from the pistol range before this interview. The Afghani doctor did not save the bullet because shootings in Afghanistan were still not a police reportable matter.

"Have you ever heard of Eymuhbad, before?" I asked jabbing a thumb at Tommy. "Because if you did, I really don't think that story about him bursting a man's skull open with his bare hands is true. Think about it. This bone is pretty tough stuff. Now that one story where he burst the guy's skull opens using a couple of rocks...? That story...that one I believe."

"I'll tell you something else, this MP carves his initials into every bullet so there is no arguing who shot who. As you can see, the initials JS are on the side of this bullet, for John Swanson. Now, I'm going to put it to you as plain as I can. I believe him, and I don't believe you. You have information I want, and my file here says you are a tough nut to crack." I saw his ego inflating, at the same time his fear ran deeper, through the very fabric of his soul.

"It says here, you are pretty tough. We have you as a suspect in many things but we just haven't been able to get the goods on you, so to speak." Stroke that ego. Show him how incompetent you are.

"Now I'm here to tell you Abu, that's why my friend, Eymuhbad is here."

"What are you? You are good cop? He is bad cop?" Abu said, grinning. Thinking that he had it all figured out.

In a quiet, calm voice, I said, "Boy did you misread this whole situation." With that, I slapped him in the face with alarming swiftness and power. The objective was not to hurt him, although that's not entirely a bad thing either, but just to scare the ever-livin' shit out of him.

"I can't believe that you are this flippin' stupid! Good Cop/Bad Cop? Those guys went to lunch years ago. Right after September 11th. No, no, no, no... What you have here is rotten-clean-through-to-the-bone-marrow-Cop and Inhumanly-Brutal Cop!" I said, jabbing my thumb at Tommy, who barely batted an eyelash since coming into the room.

"Our file on you says you're too tough to crack. That's why I am just going to turn you over to him."

"I have rights!" he cried.

"The fuck you say!" I screamed into his face. "You are not covered under the U.S. Constitution since you are not a U.S. citizen, and we are certainly not in the U.S. So, no, you don't."

"He is KGB and you...you are CIA!"

"CIA? I can't even spell it. No, I'm not CIA. Besides, they have rules too. I'm afraid you aren't that fuckin'' lucky," I said in a snarl.

"I've done nothing to the Russians," He said, tacitly admitting that he had done something.

"I don't care. The Russians had a diplomat shot a few weeks ago in Islamabad. As far as I'm concerned, you did it. As far as he's concerned, you might know who did it. Either way, we win." With that, he looked down at his feet and began rocking back and forth muttering prayers.

"Just as soon as my paperwork is ready, I'm going to hand you over, and you will be on the next train heading to KGB headquarters. Well, the FSB, now. I hear once you are there, you will either go to a gulag, or they will slowly feed you into a furnace, feet first. Now you have a nice day." With that, we both left the room.

It was all Kabuki theater. Tommy was certainly not with the FSB. I was not a colonel. He was not going anywhere. We had no file on him and knew nothing of his existence prior to this. Our hope was that he was just a low level minion. Somebody they promised some great rewards to, to pull a simple job, and now was more scared than anything else. The file I had was thick, almost bursting with carbon copies of random reports, supply forms, Xerox copies, and newspaper clippings with a few sale pages to give it some weight.

Tommy and I went for coffee. After two hours, we came back into the room and found him no longer praying. He'd made a decision which didn't involve his death. He couldn't sing fast enough when we came back to prep him for his 'final departure'. The problem being is that he was the low level minion we thought he would be, and because of that he didn't really know much.

"What is it that you want to know? I will tell you everything that I can."

"My, my...you aren't so tough after all. Let's start with your safe house in Bagram. But, the first time I catch you in a lie, you will be Moscow bound."

Abu spit out the location and drew us a map. We also squeezed him for an extremely accurate description of his contact at this location. However, as has happened so many times in the past, the Afghans will use us to tighten up old scores with anybody who has wronged them in the past—real or imagined. We had to impress upon him the importance of accurate information.

"When do you meet your contact again?"

"When I get out of the hospital. He took me to the hospital in Kabul and I'm to call him when I'm released. He has instructions to take me to a meeting where I'm supposed to receive new orders."

"Abu, we are going to confirm this information. If one shred of it doesn't pan out true, once we find your real safe house here, we'll drive you there, drop you off and hand you a stack of cash, and say, 'thanks for all the information, Abu. Call us when you can'. Look at me. You know I'm telling you the truth. You know that I will do it and you also know that whatever they do to you will be so much worse than anything we can dream up."

Abu nodded weakly. He knew I told the truth and that he had just thoroughly burned the bridge to that part of his life. They would never take him back.

It was too easy. However, the funny thing about this work is sometimes it really is just that easy—especially when you are dealing with untrained amateurs.

* * * *

22:00

Tommy and I watched Abu's safe house between houses on a parallel block. We had a camera set up on a tripod and were concealed beneath a small patch of desert camouflage netting, laying in the prone in the dark. We were able to get decent footage and still photos of everybody who came in and out the safe house, but they all moved with the sort of oblivion that desperate hunted men never seemed to achieve. Hunted men are always looking around, trying to make it look casual, but constantly on the watch. My bet was none of these were anybody we needed or even wanted at this point.

In Afghanistan, everything wraps up pretty early because nobody wants to have to travel at night. This is fine with me because, other than the occasion night like tonight, it allows me to have basically a 9:00 to 5:00 war. By our count, there was still at least one man inside the residence, and no women were observed at any point.

* * * *

22:30

The last visitor exited the house and departed on foot. I followed him around the corner and into his car up until he drove away. Getting the details I could, I returned to Tommy and told him, "That one may be worth making a note of. We have an empty street here, but he takes the time and effort to park around the corner. We have his face?"

"Yeah, some really good still photos from when he arrived and it was still light out," Tommy replied.

"Let's give him five minutes, then I'll go in and say, 'Hi'."

Tommy said, "Yeah, I'm just not feeling all that social tonight. Do you understand?"

"What's the matter, Tommy? Ya' got a little sand in your clitoris?"

"That must be it," he chuckled in response.

"Come on. Bailey used to say, 'if you couldn't kill 'em with your bare hands, you didn't want to bother'. Well, here's your chance." I egged him on because Tommy was in reality a small slender, couple years older than me, mild mannered very tofu sort of man. When I say tofu, I mean he had plenty of his sense of humor, or 'flavor', if you will, but it really only came out when there was somebody else to bounce it off of. Truth be told, I think that's why he like hanging around me.

"No Rick, thanks. I appreciate it. I really do. That's thoughtful. I already showered today, and I don't want to get all bloody again."

"You're not going to shower in the morning?"

"Yeah, but I didn't want to have to shower tonight."

"Have it your way. If anybody besides me walks out of there, call it in and follow them."

"Got it."

With that, I moved out and made my way to the house. Crouching beneath the windows, the neighbors lights were still burning, so I wasn't worried about them seeing me. Nobody appeared at the windows anyways. I stepped up the stone stairs to front door and was thankful, because stone doesn't creek. I reached for the door knob and gave it a quiet twist. It was open. Thank God for amateurs!

I cracked the door and listened; then slid inside with my Berretta out. The living room had a couple of pictures on the wall, the sort of cheesy pictures that Central Asians seemed to fancy. Portraits mostly adorned with all sorts of flowers and the room was furnished in the sort of junk collected at the curb. It had a TV and a radio was playing off in the kitchen. He was in the kitchen and I still couldn't hear any wife or kids.

I stepped into the living room and went to the wall that held the kitchen door. He came out of the kitchen walked into the living room, right past me and went to the coffee table to retrieve a tea kettle and a glass; I took one step into the middle of the living room floor. He was about 5'6", a fat balding man wearing a man dress, with a full beard and mustache and some jet black hair still remained. When he turned and saw me, he straightened up and began to say something. However, before his mouth could utter the first syllable, I fired twice. My shots were so close together some might even have thought it was one shot.

He stood frozen in fear as the glass tea cup in his left hand disappeared and the tea pot in his right hand exploded as my second bullet ripped through it. While I heard my brass bouncing on the floor, I said in a quiet voice, "Shut up!" I usually spoke in an almost whisper when I did this sort of thing, because it forced people to listen to you. The problem gets to be that a gun shot in a small confined room, has a tendency to deafen their ears for a minute. I stepped closer and he backed up. I kept stepping around, to the side. With each step I took forward, he took one back, as I angled him and stepped. I steered him to a wall where he had nowhere else to go. It had the desired effect. His face noticeably gave the look of a man trapped.

"Where are your wife and kids?"

"No wife. No kids," he said, blubbering.

"That must suck. I bet you were really looking forward to 'Man Love Thursday'," I said, making reference to the most disgusting Afghan tradition that any heterosexual western male will ever witness.

He inhaled a ragged breath. "What's your name?" I asked.

He suddenly stiffened up, defiance, he raised his jaw and

started to lean forward with indignation and yelled, "I am Mullah Mohammed Akawi and this is a Madrassa! And..."

I didn't let him finish the sentence before I pulled the trigger again. I wasn't looking down the sight during any of this, like I normally would. However, since we were only ten feet apart, I thought it superfluous. That might explain why this bullet was an inch or two closer than I had intended, however I wasn't at all disappointed with the effect. Before the pistol had finished its recoil, I watched a hole suddenly sprout in the adobe wall about an inch from his left ear. He gave up his protest and clapped his hands to his ear, fearing that I had shot it off. He held the side of his head and sobbed uncontrollably.

It was a very long moment before he felt brave enough to take his hands down to check for blood. I grabbed him by the face and screamed at him, "I'm not fuckin'g stupid and you're no Mullah! Now, if you lie to me again, I will take your ear off!" I pushed his head back against the wall and he left his hands up high, quivering above his shoulders. I watched his wild frenzied eyes start to stabilize while his lower lip continued to quiver like his hands. There was no faking this sort of terror. However, I also knew that it would be short-lived.

"You housed a man here a few days ago, Abu Said Lamas. What were your instructions for him?"

Still blubbering, "I was to give him anything he needed and then, after his mission, in two weeks time, I was to drive him to Jallallabad where we would meet up with several others, and they would receive instructions there. I was also to provide him with 50,000 Afghanis and $10,000.00 in U.S. dollars."

"Where's the money you were supposed to give him?"

"There in the cabinet..." he said pointing with a still quivering finger. I backed up then motioned him forward and gestured him to open the cabinet. I step back, look inside for a surprise, then I told him to stack the money on top of the table. It was all U.S. Dollars, perhaps a million in total of varying denominations—all of it banded and wrapped in plastic seals.

"Back up against the wall." He complied without question or protest.

"What else do you know, Mohammed?"

"I don't know anything else..."

I didn't ask twice. Again the wall behind him sprouted another hole, an inch from his right ear this time and I listened to the sound of my brass bouncing on the adobe floor. His hands and arms flew up to cover his head while he stamped his feet and made whining, mewing sounds. He stamped his feet in a circle as though he might piss his pants. I didn't care. It wasn't my floor.

Again, pure unmitigated panic wracked him.

"Okay, here's how this works. When I find out that you are holding out on us, I'll probably kill you. And I will find out, sooner or later. Of that much, you can be certain. Somehow. Someway. Someday. I will most definitely kill you. However, if you tell anybody else that I was here, you can be certain that your friends will kill you, because they won't believe that I didn't turn you into an asset for us. There are two certain things here. Squeal and you'll be dead. Lie to me, and you'll be dead. The best way for you now is to accept my very gracious offer of allowing you to see the sun rise for another day."

For the next two hours, he answered every question I put to him, no bullshit allowed. Upon completion of our conversation, I explained to him the simple mathematics that he is more valuable to me alive, for the moment, rather than dead. I also stressed the words, 'for the moment'. I took the cash from him, leaving him with a hundred thousand, in case he had other disbursements to make in the interim.

I made my way around out the back door, and sat in what should've been a back yard, while I listened to the sights and sounds of the neighborhood. I stayed perfectly still for twenty minutes, listening for the slightest sound untoward. There were none. I then took a very roundabout way back to Tommy. All in all, it was a very productive day.

* * * *

Friday, 13:00

We took Wednesday to do our paperwork and I had a great deal of intelligence resulting from my conversation with Mohammed. This took up most of Thursday.

Friday however, the Brigadier took about thirty minutes to go over the facts and the information developed to ensure that he had a clear intelligence picture, as it existed to date. He closed the files and slid them back across the desk at us, then said "I guess you are going to Mehtar Lam. Tommy will stay here to go with Mohammed and Abu when they make their link up."

"I don't see why we need to do this, Sir. This is an operation involving a hostile Intelligence Service's plans to conduct attacks or in some way harm the United States and her allies. That makes it a counterintelligence CI matter, and I'm not a counterintelligence agent. That means I can go back to Alpha Company; after all, I'm an intelligence collector," I said, putting emphasis on the word collector. This was my way of saying, 'Hey Sir, I'm really not an Intelligence weenie! I'm an action figure.'

"Give it to Tommy," I said, much to his chagrin.

"The fact of the matter is the Taliban are conducting operations against the U.S. and her allies. Of which, I count myself as one. However, since they really have no defined intelligence service, and certainly no defined uniform or boundaries, or established sovereignty, it's both an Intelligence and Counterintelligence matter. Enjoy Mehtar Lam."

"Give it to Tommy *who was now trying so hard to be invisible*; he's a CI Agent *not to be confused with the CIA. The Army has Counterintelligence agents assigned to the Counterintelligence Corps, or CIC*, furthermore he needs something to do."

"The fact of the matter is Burns, er...Rick—*he used my first name? I braced myself for that penetrating impact that was surely inbound*—nobody else will work with him due to his ah... personality disorder."

"You mean his lack thereof? A personality?"

"Precisely."

"Sir, that money we recovered from Mohammed's place was all counterfeit, why don't we through this bone to the U.S. Secret Service?"

"Because I was so informed by your Deputy Secretary of the Treasury last night that the Secret Service has an extremely limited charter beyond the Continental U.S. In fact, those were his exact words, and he repeated again, for my benefit, extremely limited. Besides, I know you really don't want to hunker down behind the sand bags, trading bullets with Al Qaeda. You can have the weekend here in Bagram, and then leave Monday. You're a collections man, now go out there and collect some Intelligence."

Tommy asked, "You wanna go grab dinner?"

My eyes had found Moneypenny, walking into the break room with her tea cup and I felt the need to address something. No, it wasn't her grooming habits, but it did spring from that. "Yeah, that's a good idea, but can you give me five minutes?"

"Sure, I'll go lock up these files," and he was gone. I headed for the break room and Moneypenny specifically. When I stepped inside, she was standing at the counter letting her tea steep. I took in all of the splendor and beauty that *was*, Moneypenny. Despite the heat, she always dressed professionally. She didn't wear athletic or polo shirts as was the custom of civilians, or khaki vests. She always wore Docker slacks and a nice button down blouse. I was marveling at her tremendous pear shaped rump and the way that her torso took off at such sharp angles from her narrow waist. She frequently wore her long hair in a pony tail, but at the end of the day, like now, most of the time, she shook it loose, and it hung down to the middle of her back. I don't know how she could tolerate it in this heat.

I tried to sound as casual as possible, "Moneypenny, I wanted to talk to you alone for a minute, do you have some time?"

She turned and looked at me over her shoulder, "Ah, yes... Alone...? Oh, for you? Are you sure you want to just...*talk*?"

"Yes, I'm sure." Then I reconsidered that answer, "For now, anyways."

"Well, it would appear that I have at least four and a half months. What can I do for you? Or...Heaven forbid, *to* you?"

"Actually, it's that specifically that I wanted to talk about."

"And what's that? *To you*, or *for you*?"

"Precisely." I decided to play her game for a few minutes, perhaps even raise the ante a little, "Why does one have to be exclusive of the other?" I asked.

She raised an eyebrow, "Well, you bring up a very good point. They don't have to be exclusive. I suppose it depended on just what, or perhaps, whom you wanted..."

"Yes, I suppose so." I stood beside her at the counter beside the coffee maker while she turned around facing the direction from which I'd just entered the room.

"Well, what specifically was on your mind?" She leaned back resting against the counter and brought her tea cup up to her lips, bracing her other hand on the counter. I noticed that she arched her back slightly and filled her diaphragm, expanding her fantastic chest undeniably and deliciously. *God Bless her! She knew exactly what was on my mind now!*

I poured myself a half cup and also turned to stand beside her facing the same way. "I was wondering what we were doing here. Mind you I love the little banter and double enchantress. It's just that you know I'm a married man, and I can only assume that for some reason, I am a safe target for your...need to tease, or an outlet for your pent up frustrations? Am I right?"

She never spoke to anybody the way that she spoke to me. In

fact, quite the opposite, I'd already hear her say on two occasions to men she'd caught staring at the bounty of her breasts, "Hey! I'm up here..."

Moneypenny looked at me sideways and said, "Well, I suppose it would really only be teasing, if I wasn't prepared to follow through on my actions or stated intent. Besides, who teases you today? Certainly not me?" *So, she wants to play it coy. Fine with me.*

"Oh, not you? There was no discussion this morning of shaving?"

"What makes you think I wasn't talking about my legs?"

Now I felt like an imbecile. She was right. I'd jumped to conclusions, filled in the rest of the sentence with my own words. No, don't give up so fast Rick; you have her on the defensive, keep her there.

"Oh, so you were discussing your legs, were you?"

She smiled wryly, "No, I wasn't."

"I didn't think so."

"I guess I like you," she whispered. She then leaned in closer and became very conspiratorial, "Because you are safe. Because it's important to me to feel desirable, not to forget that I am a woman."

"I shouldn't think that would be a problem here. I know you must see how everybody looks at you."

"Yes I do, and I know that I have a nice figure, but most of those drooling idiots only see the body and want the body. They don't know me, like me or much less, *respect* me."

"I can tell you do. I knew from the first moment I met you."

"How's that?"

"Because you looked me in the eye when we shook hands. Most men won't look above my shoulders. I like you Master Sergeant and you seem like a fun person to play with. What's more is, I respect you too. Most analysts always think they are the smartest people in the room. They think of people like you as trigger pulling, trained monkeys. Yes, I genuinely like you."

"Well, thank you but I like baseball and dogs, too." I stood up straight and made like I was about to leave.

"Oh, trust me, that's not what I meant when I said 'I like you'. I want you to know I am here to help you...in *any* way that I can... with *all* of your *wants, needs and desires*..."

When I first met her, I'd felt an "unmistakable" attraction between the two of us. I say "unmistakable", because it's very mistakable. I've misread that feeling a couple of dozen times. However, since I'm married now, I just don't act on it. It really is just that simple. However, my guess was that Moneypenny, in her need to feel desirable, chose somebody who works outside the office, so as not to complicate matters inside the office. Since I work outside...I really think this is all a bluff. That when push came to shove, she would back out of everything all together, feign some sort of terrible misunderstanding. She wanted to play a game of Sexual Chicken. I was now sure of it.

Here, now, I stepped back toward the counter, and covered her hand with mine, her eyes betrayed a slight look of surprise that I might actually act out on her words. She had started something here, and I didn't want her to think that she had me blushing and running for cover at her every presence. No, I had to go on offense.

"Well, Moneypenny. I want you to know the same thing," I began lightly stroking her palm and held her hand in mine loosely. "That I am every bit as good a friend as you are." Our fingers now gently intertwine and brush each others. Her eyes looked to mine, confused, almost pleading. "I am always willing to help you, with *your wants, needs and desires*."

Then I stepped around and stood directly in front of her and she pushed off of the counter and put her tea cup down, standing straight, straddling the foot I had placed between hers. With a couple of three inch steps, she had closed the distance between us, and she now held my hand in both of hers between our bodies. I felt her hips begin the slightest snuggle against mine. I could feel the slight bulge of her mounds as she placed it against my groin. Her eyes suddenly looked glassy and she tilted her head slightly as her face inched forward. Closing the distance between our mouths by half...

"Hey Rick, are you ready to go?" asked Tommy, standing at the door.

Moneypenny's whole disposition changed in an instant, as she suddenly brought my hand up in both of hers as if she were shaking it, "Well, it's so very good to know that you and I are on the same page regarding this matter, Richard, or do you prefer Rick?" She made very pronounced shakes of my hand, seeming to deliberately brush my against her breasts with each shake, very plainly no less than four times. *Heavenly...accident, or not?*

"We'll stick with Richard, and you don't mind? Being called Moneypenny, that is?"

"Oh, no. She was always one of my favorite characters in the old Bond movies. Well, I see Sergeant Allen is here to collect you, therefore, I won't keep you. I'll see you in the morning."

"Good night Moneypenny." *Well, in our game of bare knuckles "Sexual Chicken Master of the Universe," I think it was at best, a draw. But, I got a feel! Albeit, only with the back of my hand, but a feel, at this stage is still a feel! I'm such a dog. No! A pig. There could be no doubt, I am a pig!*

Chapter Three

Week ending 8/8/09
Monday, 19:00

I flew from Bagram to Mehtar Lam via CH-47 helicopter this is one of the large twin rotor type helicopters that have such an amazing lift capability. There were four of us bound for Meth the shortened term for Mehtar Lam, but only one of us with a specific Intelligence mission. The other three were Captain Ron Livingston, Specialist Derek Westly and Sergeant First Class Mike "Krash" Simpson.

* * * *

Tuesday, 01:00
After undergoing the usual nut-roll of changing aircraft and getting all the manifested passengers and baggage squared away, we finally took off at 22:00. This got me into Meth at 01:00, and in bed by 02:00.

* * * *

09:00
I got myself acquainted with my new digs. A pretty tiny little firebase about an hour's drive North and West of Jallallabad. The four people I flew in with were all assigned to the Afghan Public Protection Force APPF, which is a Special Forces Mission designed to recruit and train Police Officers at the Local level, making them similar to a county sheriff's deputy or a village police officer. Their training academy was located at 'the Lam' this was our dig at the Vietnam vets who always referred to their time in country as, 'the Nam', and to get a better feel for my surroundings, I rode with them for the next couple of days and took a look at their training facility, barracks, classrooms, etc.

We were all taken with the quarry that was located about two miles outside, northwest of the firebase. Blasting for rock at night? Blasting for rock in Afghanistan? The blasting also had a muffled sound to it, too. Not at all like the crisp crack of American made explosives or demolitions. Probably Home Made Explosives HME.

* * * *

Wednesday, 11:00
I knew one Interrogator at Mehtar Lam who had been a Rifleman in the Marine Corps before joining the Army, this was Christoper Marshall. I asked Chris to accompany me, in civilian clothes and introduce to me to the local village elder. Contrary to popular belief, these interrogators are highly trained and skilled professionals. Much better at the psychology aspects of questioning than I am.

We also took with us an Interpreter, or 'terp' as they are called. Only class III terps with a valid security clearance were authorized to be involved in any Special Forces or Intelligence related activities. When it's a Special Forces Intelligence mission...well, that must be ultra Top Secret—Destroy before reading. We found one that Chris had worked with before and trusted.

We met with a grizzled old man, who looked older than seventy years old. In Afghan years, this guy had to be close to a thousand. In reality, he was probably less than sixty. I asked him about the recent upturn in violence in the province. He said that Al Qaeda is like ants, and that they swarm all over Afghanistan, and that the swarm has moved to their village.

I asked him, "Where do I find this ant colony?"

He said that I "should look to where I hear them, at the quarry."

Chris and I stopped at and talked to every home on that street for two blocks, just so anybody watching us would have to guess who really said anything.

* * * *

14:00
We went to the local Bazaar, mostly curious to see how it compared to the one in Bagram. The Bagram bazaar has scaled down a lot, since my last vacation in '03. Nowhere near as much neat stuff. Either way, I had the time, so I took the time. Putting on some civilian clothes, so as not to draw any unwanted attention, I went to town.

This bazaar didn't have so much neat military stuff either but, a better selection and far better prices than Bagram. Of course, haggling is still the order of business. I took a second to notice three military aged males in man-dresses standing and talking at the corner of a building and who showed no interest in doing any shopping. The oldest among them was about age fifty. All of them seemed to be engaged in the favorite Afghan past-time, just a lot of smoking, talking and pointing. Essentially, nothing.

I was looking at a boot-legged copy of *Star Trek* when everything went silent and I suddenly found myself staring at the sky, while I saw a large brown cloud of dust creeping up towards the clouds, through the peripheral vision of my right eye. Stunned for just a second, I rolled over and drew my Berretta then surveyed the scene. The three military aged males were now two in number and were looking around the corner of the building, and one of them had wires in his hand and was squatting down holding the wires to a motorcycle battery, the wires went to the ground and ran in the general direction of a Toyota, that had its entire ass end blown off and was still burning.

"Gotchya!" I thought to myself. I stood up and made my way to the building on their side of the street, and began moving toward them. Pandemonium was going on in the street. It looked as though it had been a Vehicle Bourn Improvised Explosive Device VBIED, judging from the Toyota that was now black and burning. Either they didn't use enough explosives or some of it failed to detonate. Four armored Hummers rolled up to the scene from the firebase and two MP's from the first vehicle dismounted, grabbed their weapons and began to take stock of the damage.

I could only see five or six relatively minor wounded, three children with what looked to be cuts from flying glass, two older heavy women with the same, and one old man who appeared dazed and confused with bleeding from his head. Nothing looked life threatening. I saw Chris and his terp helping with the wounded, rendering first aid, so I continued with my task at hand. I slid along the wall toward my two targets. I managed to grab the eye of one of the MPs and I flagged him over. He brought his partner and flattened out against the wall with me.

"I got two guys on the end of this block. I saw one of them was holding wires to a motorcycle battery a second after the detonation. I think they were probably waiting on you, but just got too anxious. Let's go talk to them," I said to the young Specialist who was nearest me. His partner, a Private First Class PFC, was leaning around him, staring at me intently, hanging on my every syllable.

"Who are you?" the Specialist asked.

I said simply, "Intelligence."

We slid along the wall until we were just a few yards away. I gave the two MPs a hold still motion with my hand and I leveled my pistol with both hands and gradually side stepped away from the building, scooting just three or four inches at a step, until both of them were in line with the muzzle of my handgun. I began stepping towards them since they still hadn't noticed me. When I was a couple of yards away, one of them looked me in the eyes, and panicked. He slapped his friend on the shoulder and the two of them took off. I was hot on their heels, and one of them stumbled and I was on him, I shoved him to the ground and kept running after the one in the lead. The nearest MP behind me grabbed 'stumbles' and knelt on his back while his partner and I did our best to keep Stretch the taller of the two in sight. The MP was completely laden in forty pounds of body armor and another twenty-five pounds of ammunition, and probably another ten pounds of radio, and water. He was doing his best, God Bless him.

Stretch lost his flip-flop sandals a few hundred yards back and was now running bare foot and had a pistol in his hand. When he got to the end of the last block he stopped running and turned to face me and raised his weapon. I was still almost fifty yards back and wasn't particularly worried that he would hit me.

He was out of breath, he was stressed, he had horrible training, and the distance was too great. I slowed and brought my weapon to bear, and at that very second, I heard the MP behind me yell, "Stop! Drop that..." Stretch suddenly shifted his weapon from me to the MP, and blam! Blam! "...gun!"

I turned to look behind me and saw the MP with his M-16 rifle braced against the side of a building, shaking like a leaf, sweating profusely, eyes the size of pie plates. I gave him a wave of my hand and moved forward to check out Stretch.

I picked up his pistol, a piece of shit that wouldn't get $10.00 at a pawn shop, then I felt for his carotid pulse. One beat, two beats, three beats...then nothing. He looked about twenty-five years old, but it's hard to tell sometimes with Central Asians. I went back to the MP who was still wide eyed in shock and almost hyperventilating. I took his mouthpiece to his camelback back worn water source, replaced the canteen and fed it to him. If he's anything like me, soon, he'll be so thirsty he couldn't possibly carry enough water to satisfy that thirst.

We checked the body for any additional devices. There were none. So we made our way back to the 'Stumbles'.

"Nice shooting, Specialist," I said. "Come on, let's go check on your partner."

"Thanks," he mumbled in reply.

That MP had already had him bound in flex-cuffs and still had one knee on his back. He was squirming and protesting, "What do you want with me? I didn't do anything."

He had a point. It was Stretch that I had seen with the detonator. The MP who had cuffed him up said simply, "You are being detained for further investigation." MP don't have any arrest authority, only Commissioned Officers can place somebody "under arrest."

"Are you okay, Steve?" The PFC asked his partner, doubtlessly having heard the shots.

Steve shook his head 'yes' but said nothing else.

* * * *

15:30

Sitting in the holding cell at the MP station at the firebase, I was explaining a few things to 'Stumbles,' "Look, I saw you with the man who detonated the device both before and within seconds of the blast. You will be determined to be an Unlawful Enemy Combatant. That much is certain. In the morning, I'll be taking you to the Bagram Detention Facility." The terp yammered what I had just said in Pashto to him.

The kid, of about seventeen or eighteen merely nodded his head in understanding.

"I want to ask you something. Don't worry. Anything you tell me right now will not be used against you in any legal proceedings. This is what we call 'off the record'; do you understand?" The terp yammered again.

He nodded his head 'yes,'

"Where did you receive your training?"

Through the terp, the kid responded one word only, "Quarry."

"How many were in your group?"

"Only six." He held up six fingers for me. "The teacher, who was with us at the bazaar, wants to get much bigger classes, and is hoping to recruit more once he is stronger. But we are his first class."

"Okay, all. We are back on the record now. Everything you say from this moment forward, WILL be used against you. That was it. Do you understand?" The terp yammered.

"Yes," he said himself. So, the kid knew at least some English.

* * * *

16:00
Chris and I walked out the wire and made our way through the maze of mud huts towards the quarry. I wanted to get into position before dark, and before they turned on the huge standing tower lights they had. Few things in life are certain. But Chris being a former Rifleman and therefore knew how to "ditty-bop," in the bush, and knew how to handle himself in a nice bare-knuckles brawl, were two of these certainties.

We now had what is called "Actionable Intelligence." Meaning we had developed some raw information and confirmed it through another source. Ideally, we would've confirmed it through a different vehicle, such as imagery or electronics. What we had was enough.

I left Chris at the last lane of mud huts with instructions to call me on the radio if anybody tried to follow me. With that, I flipped over the shroud of my ghillie suit, laid in the prone firing position, and slowly crawled my way up hill, the last thousand meters to the edge of the quarry.

* * * *

18:00
In my early years, when I was an Infantry Sergeant in the 82nd Airborne Division, I was selected and went to the Special Forces Sniper Course. That was twenty-seven years ago. Long before I went to Special Forces and long before I sold my soul to the Intelligence beast.

I'm not the same man I was in those days for a multitude of reasons. That was the type of man needed tonight, so this is the man I would have to be. Again.

I assumed a position above the quarry, which afforded me an excellent view of the road leading from the top, all the way to the bottom. The road was perhaps 900 meters away, and the farthest portion of the quarry floor approximately 700 meters. Not a soul was in sight. I noticed my breathing was much faster and it wasn't all from the crawl. I began my series of exercises to slow my breathing and heart rate.

* * * *

19:08
A gray Toyota Hilux pickup truck was seen driving down the road from the top of the quarry with three passengers in addition to the driver. Once they were at the quarry floor, I could identify the third man from the bazaar that I had seen earlier with Stretch and 'Stumbles'. He was waving his arms wildly and speaking in loud tones which I heard faintly, despite the distance. He appeared to be the instructor in the crowd, perhaps fifty to fifty-five years old. Everybody else was at least between twenty-five and forty years old.

Ten minutes later, another Hilux was seen driving down the road towards the bottom with a driver and two passengers. I slowly and quietly unfolded the bipod legs of my M-21 sniper system *yeah, it's old, but it still works.* Now, I was bathed in sweat. The pressure was always intense.

The reason I had the M-21 was because the Brigadier thought this would be the better option than involving a larger direct action force, like a twelve man Special Forces Operational Detachment-Alpha SF-ODA or a sixteen man Navy SEAL platoon. So in a way, I was just warming up for an upcoming operation. The sun was down now but glowing below the horizon and it would soon be dark and the lights would come on. I looked through the scope of my rifle and did another range estimate in my head using the stadia lines cross hairs in the scope. Then I proceeded to watch as the instructor brings his students together and shows them the intricacies of the DuPont box, this is the "plunger" or detonating device which generates an electrical charge to the blasting cap, named for DuPont who won the Nobel Prize for the invention of dynamite.

There was a crane and a bulldozer at the bottom of the quarry. Old Russian pieces of shit. Nobody made any moves to start any machinery, or equipment. Not the crane, not the dozer, not a dump truck. Nobody was there to do any quarry work. This was a bomb making class about to be in session.

* * * *

19:21

Say Good Night

I was loosing light fast.

The driver of the second vehicle broke from the group and started the generator near the shack at the base of the quarry. Within a minute, the entire quarry was bathed in glowing bright light. I could feel the sweat flowing freely from me now.

As if to make some kind of point, the instructor raised his arms to shoulder height and turned 360 degrees to show everybody how bright it was, or how vast his power was, or some other such crap.

Now came the stingingly cold blooded aspect of this job. It's cold-blooded, because at that precise moment, before action commences, you're shooting a man who is no real imminent threat to you, specifically. Furthermore, I positioned myself a good 200-300 meters beyond the maximum effective range of their rifles, provided they didn't have anything bigger than your garden variety Russian AK. You have to be able to accept the solace that comes with the knowledge that he would kill Americans on another day. All of them would. They would all happily march us down to the train stations and load us all on to cattle cars haul us away, then march us right up to delousing. You, me, all of our children and grandchildren. Well, not today. I made a note of the time, 19:21; Start of action. Either way, I had decided that it was time for them to die.

The pressure completely enveloped me now. It was stifling and oppressive, breathing was difficult as my chest was so tight. I felt the old familiar tension headache, come on instantly. It always felt as if my head were clamped in a vice. Despite the relatively pleasant eighty degrees, I was now soaking wet with sweat.

I lifted the weapon, took a second to dry my sweaty hands on my sleeves, deep breaths, then I took a reading of my winds. They were very light, maybe two to four knots, and they were at my back, no value *to a sniper, 'no value' winds are winds that do not require any sight or hold adjustments*. Down in the quarry they would probably be non-existed. I couldn't see any dust flying anywhere in the kill zone. A straight on simple shot. *How often does that happen*, I asked myself. *Not much. Never mind that, they're targets, nothing more, and it's just another day on the range*, I coached myself. *Breathe deep, steady, in... out... line 'em up. Come on, Sweet Cheeks. Let me see your smile. Turn a little more. Steady hand, smoooth squeeeze... Now say, 'Good night',* ka blam! The rifle punched against my shoulder. The old familiar feeling felt hauntingly good.

My God! I'm so thirsty!

I was still watching through the scope, when the bullet struck him a second and a quarter later. Square in the chest and he dropped like a stone. It never fails. I'm always amazed by how quickly they drop, how suddenly they fall, if you can call it a fall. Once a man is struck with a single killing shot, they just seem to throw themselves down. The finality of it is all so...striking. *Binos! Get your binos acquire another target Binos being Army speak for Binoculars.*

The second driver was now running back towards the generator to kill the lights. *Not yet. Take your time, you have all the time in the world, now...steady. Squeeeze... Say 'Good night',* ka blam! I felt that punch from the stock. This wasn't as good of a shot, he pitched forward on to his face, I saw the red stain growing over his back, as he pushed himself up on all fours, I fired again and took his left elbow out from underneath him, he pitch forward back on to his face. He pushed his way up to his knees again with his right arm and began walking on his knees toward the generator. *I wish he hadn't done this, look so pathetic, show determination and a desire to stay alive.* I fired again. *Say 'Good night',* ka blam! With finality, he was flung to the ground, again onto his face. Only this time, never to move again.

The remaining four sought cover behind the two vehicles, one of them pulled an AK-47 from inside the Hilux and began firing wildly at the edge of the quarry wall in my general direction. He must've felt the AK made him bullet proof, emboldened him because he stood tall and walked from behind the vehicle, just stitching the tops of the quarry walls. Nothing even came close to me. *Line it up...breathing, in...out...in...out...relax. It's just another shot. Relax. Come on, Sweet Cheeks, smile big... Say 'Good night',* ka blam! I felt that comfortable punch of the rifle in recoil. He dropped like a stone, never to move again.

Binos! Go to your binos, find the next one. So fuckin' thirsty!

One of the final three, ran towards the crane and attempted to start it up. I think his intention was to scrape me off of the edge of the quarry. Provided he had a real good fix on my position *and I doubted it*, not a bad thought, but I also knew that crane probably wouldn't extend from the bottom of the quarry to the edge where I was. Kind of creative though. He climbed into the cab, when he sat back in the seat, I fired. He remained seated but he wasn't moving. I fired again. His body lurched with the impact of that bullet. I fired again and gradually, his body slid out of the seat and down the side of the crane and onto the treads, then onto the ground, where he never moved again.

God! This headache! I'm so friggin' thirsty. I'll take some water after the next shot. Dry your hands. Get your breathing under control. Look through your binos. Relax. One of the remaining two tried to make a break for the generator again. He was running, but fast, and he was almost in line with my direction of fire so he would not be running across my field of view, of course, this also meant that I wouldn't have to lead him either. *Awww...don't try running Sweet Cheeks, you'll only die tired*, I thought to myself. I fired. He leaped over the body of the second driver, and the very instant that his toe touched the ground again my bullet tore into his back just to the left of his right shoulder blade. His upper body twisted and continued forward while his lower body showed no further interest in going that way. He struck the ground with his right side, then rolled onto his back, then... he never moved again.

The last man decided to make a break for it. He climbed inside the Hilux and I was surprised when it started up for him. Sitting and crouching in the driver's seat of a right hand 'English' drive Hilux, he was in the side of the vehicle towards me, and in the bright lights, he was a fantastic target, he tried to put the truck in gear... "Say 'Good night...'" Ka blam! He never moved again.

I made a mental note of the time. End of action; 19:28. It was too dark to make any notations on my log book. I would have to do that when I got back. By 19:30, I noticed that my headache was almost gone entirely. All that remained was a minor dull ache at the base of my skull. I turned to leave and I muttered down into the quarry, "Good night Cocksuckers." As suddenly as it arrived, my headache was gone. But...*Oh, My God! I'm so damned thirsty!*

* * * *

21:00
As dark as it was now, I didn't have to crawl my way back down from the quarry's edge. When I finally got back to Chris' location in the last mud hut, I had to crawl inside and get into a corner and then just sit and shake while the kinetic energy and stress left my body. I found myself on my knees, rocking forward and backward very much the same way that Abu had at Bagram. My hands were shaking so badly I couldn't light a cigarette, Chris had to do it for me.

I hadn't left a single survivor on the battlefield. The Army pays on the average, between seven and nine cents per round of 7.62mm ammunition. For the M-118 National Match Grade ammunition, used by snipers, this costs approximately thirteen cents per round. I fired ten rounds of match grade 7.62mm ammunition, making a total cost to the taxpayers of $1.30 cents. A very cost efficient night's work. That thought didn't ease my stress any, though.

About twenty minutes later, I had stopped shaking enough to start walking back. My legs felt like rubber and my feet seemed to slap the ground, and each step hurt my joints.

* * * *

22:00
Chris and I presented ourselves to the back gate back at the firebase. The MP opened the pedestrian gate and asked, "Who are you guys."

"Intelligence," I replied. He nodded a knowing nod and said nothing else. 'Intelligence,' that reply covers a plethora of sins. It answers a thousand questions without actually answering any of them. It always seems to stop any further questions, and those were the last things I wanted right now.

Chris asked, "What do you think was going through their minds in those final moments?"

"I don't care. I can't care. I don't dare personalize it to that degree. Otherwise, I'd never be able to do it."

* * * *

Thursday, 10:00
I really wasn't sure if there were any ties between the crowd at the quarry and the developments that I was currently working on in Bagram. I was prepared to write off the happenings at the quarry as a field-expedient expenditure in *crime prevention*.

I dropped my prisoner at Bagram Detention Facility at 9:30 and was now at the Joint Intelligence Operations Center.

I was pouring myself a cup of coffee as Moneypenny walked in and began making herself a cup of tea. I knew as soon as I spoke to her, a very sexually alluring comment was coming my way. To tell you the truth, I was burning with curiosity as to what it would be so when a flock of Intelligence 'weenies,' analysts and computer nerds and 'squints,' imagery analysts are typically called squints from squinting and staring at photos for hours on end, walked into the break room, I paused and decided that I didn't want any conversation with them.

"So, Moneypenny, how has life been treating you since I left?" She turned to verify the face and gave me a warm smile and a brief hug, lest anybody see us. Then her face took on a scowl and she went back to her seeping tea.

"Well, actually given the state you left me in, very much the way a baby treats a diaper. You were a very naughty boy when last we met. And…well…you had me in such a *mood*."

She slammed the counter top in obvious frustration, "Life will be treating me much better once the PX gets another shipment of C cell batteries!" As rare as a Big Foot sighting, I saw Moneypenny suddenly become embarrassed. She brought her hand to her mouth as though she'd said something she shouldn't have. She looked at me in wide eyed-horror and blushed.

"Err…uuhh…I mean…"

"For your reading light," I offered.

She laughed aloud, "Yes! Exactly! For my reading light!" She echoed.

"After all, it can be most…distressing when you can't read before bed," I offered.

"Precisely! I always read before going to sleep. How did you know?"

I thought about it for a second, "I guess…because we all do it."

She smiled brightly, which was all that more in contrast to her brilliant red blush.

She placed her hand at my shoulder and said, "Thank you."

I suddenly started laughing. Uncontrollably laughing. Quietly, but my shoulders shook as I was laughing so hard. Then the laughing became sobbing, and tears rolled down my cheeks. I didn't feel as though I were crying. There were no tears, but my body was racked, shaking and sobbing. Clearly some residual stress was working its way out.

Moneypenny, put her hand to my neck and asked, "Are you all right?"

I nodded but was still unable to speak as the spasms and fits continued to rack my body. Moneypenny wrapped both arms around my neck and pulled me in for a tight hug.

She whispered to me, "No, you're fine. You're here now." Around us, the weenies continued their animated discussion of the latest game gear. "Just relax, Richard. You're here, do you understand? With me. You're alright. You're just fine Rick."

And I was. Just as suddenly as I started laughing, I stopped. I wiped tears away, and I was fine again. That stress will come out some how. Everybody deals with it differently. As my fits passed, Moneypenny released me.

"I'm sure the Brigadier will want to see you." I let Moneypenny lead the way to his office.

"Ahhh, Master Sergeant! Good to see you. Productive day yesterday, huh? Pretty exciting too, I gather. With the IED and your prisoner."

"Yes Sir. That's exactly the adjective I would use. Productive."

He gave me a come here wave of his fingers as he closed his own door. "Have you had a chance to get re-acquainted with that equipment, I sent you out with?" He was referring to the sniper system. He knew that I would've had to 'zero' the scope to the rifle and get familiar with it again.

"Yes Sir, I did. I got quite a bit of time with the system."

"Would you know anything about a quarry out to the west of your firebase?"

"Only that it exists."

"Well, it would seem that the ANP Afghan National Police found quite a few dead bodies there this morning. Would you know anything about that?"

"No, I hadn't heard a thing about it, other than what the prisoner told me, about that being the place he received his demolitions training at."

"Well, then it's rather fortuitous that somebody cleaned that mess up then, isn't it?"

"Yes Sir. It is."

"Then you're prepared then to cover Tommy at the meeting on Saturday?"

"Yes Sir, which is a lot more than he does for me."

"After the last discussion I had with him, I doubt that will ever be a problem again. Good luck."

* * * *

Friday, 19:00
Finally back at Mehtar Lam. I had a big day tomorrow and equipment to prep. Tomorrow would be the meeting between or Bagram spy contingent: Abu and Mohammed and their control.

I was actually a little excited. Not 'going to Disneyworld excited,' but eager to get on to the next step in this little caper.

* * * *

Saturday, 07:00
Rather than inserting into the area by helicopter which always draws at least a little attention, I used what I call a Jingle Insertion. Here, the local nationals hang rows of chains from the bumpers of their trucks and paint them all sorts of bizarre pastel colors. Because the roads are barely recognizable as roads, the chains jingle heavily when going over the endless plethora of potholes.

There are always a gaggle of these trucks and drivers at the firebase who have just finished making deliveries. I grabbed one and paid him the equivalent of twenty dollars U.S., in Afghani, to drop me at a location about two kilometers or klicks from the meeting spot. I wanted to get there early to see if they had any surprises lined up in advance.

At 07:20, I gave the driver a wave good bye in the mirror, and walked to the road side. Once he made his turn and was around the bend and out of sight. I dropped. In the gully at the side of the road, I put on my ghillie suit. Shortly after that, I began the long arduous crawl and creep to the rendezvous point.

Like most snipers, I carried two rifles. Especially when I didn't have a spotter. One rifle, the M-21 for distance shots greater than three hundred meters. The other, an M-4 carbine, for inside of three hundred meters. My Berretta was for those times when it's really up close and personal. Naturally, this meant I had to carry ammunition for each of these as well. Ammo, in and of itself, was quite a load. All of my additional gear I carried in a small rucksack that I was using as a drag bag and had hooked to my belt. I won't give away anymore tricks of the trade.

* * * *

09:25
I got to the rendezvous point and there was nobody visible. There was a qalat of sorts. An adobe compound with no buildings, the sort of compound used for livestock. There were no recent vehicle tracks leading in or out. I was the first one here, and it was going to be a very long, excruciating day, baking in the sun until

the 14:00-16:00 meet time. There was a problem with that too, because these guys are never on time. I've heard it said that this is cultural, hogwash! That the more important the individual you're to meet with, the longer the wait. As though it is some statement as to your importance, that people are so willing to wait so long for your audience.

I found a piece of high ground which afforded me an excellent view of the compounds interior, about 400 meters from the gate, 500 meters from the back wall. Since there were only rocky hills in this area, I figured the meeting must be happening in the compound. *Brilliant.* I had a very long wait. I also had about five pints of water in my camel back and being an old soldier, I still carried the traditional two, one quart canteens and a single two quart bladder canteen on my small rucksack. I had hoped not to eat any MREs on this deployment, but that was no longer looking like a realistic option. I brought three just in case I got lost or wound up going into the Escape and Evasion E and E mode.

By noon, I was pretty thoroughly cooked. The temperature lying on the desert floor, with the heat radiating off of the sand had to be upwards of 140 degrees. I kept my water consumption up and the ghillie suite kept most of the sun directly off of me. However it was also another layer of clothing for all practical purposes so it hurt as much as it helped.

Since I was on an opposing slope, I had an excellent view inside the compound. At no time, were any Bedouins nomads, observed anywhere around the compound, and no vehicle traffic slowed to give it a glance. I didn't eat anything because an MRE would just make me thirsty as hell, at this point.

* * * *

13:15
My radio crackled to life as Tommy slowly came into range. "Colonel Binkus, this Major Sunovabytchz, over"

"Major Sunovabytchz, this is Binkus, go ahead."

"I think we are about fifteen hundred meters away. How does it look? Over."

"It's all clear. Nothing and nobody in sight."

"Roger."

"Are they supposed to meet inside the compound?"

"Mohammed says 'yes' that it's his usual contact point."

"Okay, have them park against the far back wall of the

compound. That'll give me the best coverage."

"Roger. They've been informed."

Within ten minutes, I saw their Hilux round the bend in the road coming from the North, then I saw the vehicle slow, and Tommy jump out of the back and start walking over land toward the compound. He was wearing a set of Man-Jams typical pajama sort of afghan clothes, a brown wool flat saucer hat, and a brown vest with a small canvas civilian rucksack. I knew after my meeting with the Brigadier, Tommy had more than a pistol today. He probably had a rifle or a carbine broken down into two parts and inside the ruck. I watched as he walked up over the hills near the roadside and then made his way down the other side toward the compound. We didn't want a third set of foot prints inside the compound when they arrived, so after pinpointing the compound's location, Tommy turned around and went back to the road, where he sat by the roadside on a small prayer rug, and took out a hookah pipe and set it on the ground. He pulled the *shamag Haji* head scarf, up around his face to help conceal his pale complexion, then he crossed his legs and sat down, becoming, for all intents and purposes, a stoned out old man begging for alms.

We didn't know which direction they would come from, but we hoped that it wouldn't be the North Tommy's direction. I kind of suspected that they would come from Jallallabad, the east. Either way, I would tell him when they arrived. Tommy had a wire on Mohammed and was monitoring all of their conversation. At least I hoped that he was.

"Major Sunovabytchz, are you receiving those guys?"

"Yeah, I've got 'em. Loud and clear."

"I'll give you a heads up when somebody arrives."

So it went for another four and half hours.

* * * *

17:42

Ten hours in the sun. With the sun going down it was now slightly cooler. Probably only 125 degrees, now. *How refreshing!* It's all relative.

Another Toyota Hilux arrived from the south and turned into the compound and two individuals exited the vehicle. I sighted in on both of them to get a real good look at their faces. Tommy was listening to their chatter.

"Hey Colonel Binkus, these two new guys say that they are

supposed to meet another person at the place, too, in order to received new instructions.

* * * *

17:50
A third vehicle, a Ford Ranger with an extended cab and four military aged males arrived at the compound. They stopped outside the compound and one of the rear passengers exited the vehicle and walked into the compound then looked around, said something to those inside when they started to walk towards him, but he stopped them. He then walked across the road they had been driving on and he checked the road going east, towards Jallallabad. I told Tommy that he would more than likely be looking north in a minute. Tommy packed up his wears and scurried up the hillside towards the compound. He was quickly out of sight in the rocks.

Apparently satisfied with his view to the east, the new arrival walked to the bend going north and saw nothing there. He walked back to the Ford and spoke with the other rear passenger, then climbed in. They drove into the compound and all four climbed out, looking around very sharply. The driver and other two passengers kept Mohammed and Abu and the other two at a distance until the other backseat passenger gave them the come on.

Tommy came across on the radio and I saw him coming down the hillside toward the compound. "It sounds like somebody is giving them some instructions. Where do you want me at, Rick?"

"They didn't leave anybody outside so why don't you move up towards the gate and park it on the north east corner. If anybody tries to leave, kill 'em."

"Roger," came his reply. Then I saw him climbing down the hillside towards the compound. To go with his Russian persona, Tommy was now carrying a folding stock AK-47. I watched as he moved along the outside of the north wall, then took his position at the corner.

The meeting went very quickly, and I saw him handing out packets to each of the individuals except those who came with him. The packets were large fat manila envelopes

"Hey Rick, I think the meeting is breaking up." As soon as he said it, I could feel that headache coming on. *Note the time, start of action; 17:56*. When I looked back from my watch, I locked in on the man who handed out the packets, 'Boss man,' as he started to make a turn for his vehicle and the driver reached in his pocket for the keys. I raised the rifle, lined up on the driver. *Smile nice and pretty....now...say Good night.* The rifle lurched, and the stadia lines came back down right on the driver. I watched as the bullet tore into the side of his chest cavity. I don't think he got the keys out of his pocket before he twisted, fell, then never moved again.

He went down so quickly, it had to be a killing shot. The other two passengers went just as quickly, *now, howzaboutyyou, Say Good night. And you? Good night*, in the mean time, Abu, Mohammed and the other two ran back towards their vehicles. I left only the boss man alive. I told Tommy to move inside and take him. I watched briefly as he stood up and went for the gate. He wasted no time in getting 'Boss man' flat on his face and flex cuffing him. *End of Action; 17:58.* Log book entries were made.

I folded up my bipod legs, and crawled a few meters down off of the rise and then walked down to the Jallallabad road, where I stashed my sniper system, and went in carrying my M-4. Then I walked down the road and in through the gate as bold as brass. I walked up to 'Boss man' and grabbed him by the back of his collar and yanked him to his feet. He started babbling immediately and I screamed into his face, only inches away, "Shut the fuck up!"

"First; I know you speak English. In fact, I know you studied English at the American University in Cairo." I really didn't know this, it just seems to be true so often and it was a shot in the dark.

He corrected me, "No, the American University in Beirut."

"Just as good. What's your name?"

He stuck his chest out proudly and said "I am Marid Law Watiri." As if I should know the name. He was trying to tell me that he was important and that he might be worth trading for.

The other two late arrivals were looking back and forth at each other trying to size up the situation.

"Well Marid, I'm going to assume that you are what we call in America, Middle Management. That means that you don't really get to make any decisions, just carried out the decisions of others. I'll bet a smart college educated man like you, is working for an idiot. Isn't that right?"

"No, that is not so. I work for *Allah* and all that is holy."

"Aren't you wondering how we knew you were going to be here? It was because of him," I said, pointing to the body nearest me. I picked him at random.

"He told us what an idiot you were and said your boss was even dumber. Of course, he..." I pointed to the corpse again, "...started to get a little too greedy. The information he was turning over wasn't nearly worth the money he'd been paid. Besides, he was stupid. Not very well educated. He was what we call in the U.S., Labor. You? You on the other hand, you're clearly management. After all, you studied English. Why? To defeat us! Right? Now, that's why he's laying over there, and you're sitting here talking to me right now. Don't you want to be the one making the decisions for a change?" His eyes widened, and he looked down as he pondered this new promotion opportunity. The seed had been planted, and already began to germinate.

"Look Marid, how do you think we stumbled on to Al Zarkawi? Do you think we just happened to bomb the right house for a change? No! The next in line for his job gave him up. That's how it's done. That's how it's always been done. Do you remember YaSir Arafat?"

He nodded 'yes'.

"Did you know he had seventeen million dollars in the bank when he died? How do you think he got it? It wasn't all ransoms. Now most of his money came from the French before they got wise. He kept most of it in Switzerland, some of it in France. Most everybody else had liens on his money toward the end. Now incase you're thinking that we are going to trade you, forget about it. We aren't the Italians and we certainly aren't the Israelis and going to trade a thousand prisoners for a couple of rotten corpses. No Sir, Marid. You lucked out. We are going to turn you. These four people already know we did." I said the last part pointing to the four people to whom he had just given instructions.

"Now we are going to put them on the payroll, and they will be the only people that you can trust with your secret. Now here is the beauty of the proposal. Nobody can't give up anybody else, without giving yourself up. It would be certain, horribly slooow painful death. None of you will give up the other, because nobody will believe you have not been turned as well. Security in numbers, don't ya' know?"

We had our new agent Marid went over the instructions with us, that he had just handed to everybody so we now knew where they were going and how to find them. We knew what Mohammed and Abu's part were in this scheme, but the other two who had arrived turned out to be very unexpected.

Using Marid as an interpreter, one of them said, "I am Mustafa Organahyi, I am the shipping manager for the Wazirk Paper

Company in Islamabad."

I looked to Tommy who had a very puzzled look on his face. I said in hushed tone to him, "Curiouser and curiouser, this gets."

"Who is the other man with you?"

"He is my brother. I don't know how to drive but he does."

Then for some reason, Abu felt slighted and said to me, "This man." He was pointing at Tommy, "This man. The man that you say was KGB. He does not sound like a Russian. I think maybe you lied to me. He speaks like an American."

"Eyemuhbad studied English at the American University in Moscow."

Abu's face suddenly went from angry to that expression that says "Ohhh, that makes sense." He then just nodded and stepped away.

Then we gave them all their cover story. "Okay, listen up. You met up, and you all received your instructions. However, before you could leave, the American's attacked the compound. This man here," I was pointing at the same dead body as before, "turned on you and tried to hand you over to the American troops. This man, Marid, your contact, was able to shoot a hole in the American line and using a smoke grenade then a hand grenade, he brought you through to safety where you all split up and went your separate ways. Does everybody understand?" Marid was acting as our interpreter again and they all nodded 'yes'.

I put my arm around Marid's shoulder and took him aside, almost whispering, I said, "Marid, you see how your predecessor ended up, right? You need to see that this doesn't happen to you because I can find you anywhere at anytime. I don't have to kill you outright. I can leave you crippled and alive, then walk up to you, stuff a ham sandwich in your mouth and then choke you dead. Do you understand? Would you like to meet *Allah* with a mouth full of pork?" Marid's eyes got big and he shook his head an emphatic 'no'.

"Then you need to make sure that you keep feeding us solid information. You have my numbers and you know your signals and code words, right?"

"Yes, I know exactly what to do."

"And that is, what?"

"As soon as I get back, I will tell the leaders and the security chief of my group that Petra," he jerked a thumb at the dead body I had selected earlier, "was ordered to betray us, by Nidal, my contact."

"Very good. It may take awhile for them to believe you. But your security chief will believe it instantly. The rest, maybe not right away, but they will. Eventually, they will, and then you will step into his shoes."

"What if Nidal wants to kill me before they believe me?"

"If you think he is going to hurt you, you call me and I will take care of him. Do you understand?"

"Yes, my friend. I will do as you say. As long as you take care of him, I will be grateful to you."

Chapter Four

Week ending 8/15/09
Sunday, 23:00

Tommy and I arrived at Bagram to deliver the Intelligence gathered from Marid, Abu, Mohammed and Mustafa's cell phones and copied disks that were in their instruction packets. Tommy had brought an Electronics Exploitation kit with him to the meet for just this reason. All of it Tommy copied at the compound before we sent them on their way. We'd deliver it in the morning to the exploitation team and sit down and formulate a plan in light of the recently developed intelligence.

We managed to find our way to the temporary or transient tents at Bagram, and racked out immediately. These tents are like living in steerage. Usually there are about a half dozen new terps who just arrived in country and waiting for assignments. These terps are people who are fluent in the Dari or Pashto languages who pass a preliminary background investigation by the Department of Defense DOD. Some get a much more extensive background investigation and these become level II and III terps to work with Special Forces, the Combined Joint Special Operations Task Force-Afghanistan, and the Intelligence sections at either of those posts. For the most part, they are the same people who work the register at Seven-Eleven, or drive cabs in Detroit and Chicago. Welcome home! Yeah, it sucks to be me sometimes.

* * * *

Monday, 09:00
When we arrived at the CJSOTF-A Headquarters, we simply followed the signs which read "J-2 Intelligence." As I passed Moneypenny's desk, I took advantage of her absence doubtlessly at the 09:00 'intel dump' down in the conference room, to leave a small gift wrapped present on her desk that I had picked up in Jalallabad. We continued on when we were sub-steered to the signs which read "J-2 Operations Directorate." Then lastly to the office which said simply, "Director."

The Brigadier looked over the stack of raw intelligence that we had collected from our 'meeting,' on Saturday. It was really not a bad haul. We had the disks that we had copied, all of the cell phones that we had cloned, and three new sources of up-to-date intelligence. All and all, a pretty productive trip.

"I want you both to go back to Jalallabad *aka J-Bad, Asadabad = A-Bad, Sayedabad = S-Bad, Islamabad = I-Bad,* and keep your eyes and ears on Khyber Pass and the Swat Valley. We don't know how this Paper Company in I-Bad figures into their plans but I have a feeling that is going to be key to their scheme."

Picking up on the Brigadier use of the word 'scheme,' I capitalized on it. "Yes, if we could only get to the bottom of their diabolical scheme."

"Well, yes, I suppose the word 'diabolical' does apply," the Brigadier agreed.

However, his mention of the Swat Valley and the Khyber Pass peaked my curiosity. "Why those spots, Sir? Have you heard something?"

"Yes, we collected some chatter that names those places and of course the conversation is cryptic enough to leave us guessing. So essentially, we have no idea at this point just what's going to happen there, only that something is."

For clarity, I asked, "And our mission is...?"

The Brigadier made a face and shook his head slightly, "The same as it always is: To identify the enemy. To collect intelligence on the enemy, and when the situation allows, destroy the enemy. I don't believe that I have to explain this to you."

"I'm just making sure that you don't have something specific in mind."

"I promise you Richard, if and when I do, I won't mince words. I spell it out you, in plain English."

I merely nodded.

"Tommy, you need to start cultivating some additional sources inside the Afghan Border Police. Rick, you need to stay current on your Marksmanship skills. We may have something coming up on a completely unrelated matter which might call for your expertise. Run this raw data down to the exploitation cell and let's see what we have here. Good work."

We did as we were told and dropped our collection of potential gold nuggets off at exploitation. Around 10:00 Tommy and I started to make our flight arrangements out of Bagram, using the phone at an empty desk. While Tommy was on the phone, I saw

Say Good Night

Moneypenny enter the common space work area this is similar to steerage quarters for the Intelligence weenies, where they assemble and type up all of their forecasts and analysis. Moneypenny worked in the common work area next door since she was on the Pakistan desk. I saw her make a scan of the room holding my little present tight in her hand. I turned around and tried to be invisible. About one minute later I felt her hand as she dragged her finger nails across both shoulder blades and she came around to stand in front of me. I stood up, and she wrapped both arms around my neck and gave me a very nice tight squeeze. Then with a speed that Jet Li would envy, she took me by the back of the head and pulled my face down for a kiss. Just the briefest of kisses but, a Moneypenny kiss, nonetheless. The feeling of Moneypenny's rose petal soft lips stayed there for the rest of the afternoon. *Yes, there can be no doubt; I am a pig!*

"Thank you! Thank you! Thank you! You are such a dear." *If you only knew, Moneypenny. If you only knew.*

"Well, that's sweet of you to say. What prompted that announcement?"

"Don't be silly," she held out my gift, "C Cell batteries! It couldn't have been anybody else."

"What makes you so sure?"

She looked horrified, then she leaned in closer and whispered "Because... You're the only person I said that too! What type of girl do you think I am?"

No good could come from trying to answer that question so I left it alone.

"Why did you get me so many?"

"I wasn't really sure about the dimensions or length, of your 'reading light'. I figured if I over-bought, it would give you nothing but more...pleasure...er pleasant reading, that is."

"Yes," she got a very devilish grin on her face and said, "Yes, and tonight, when I am 'reading,' I'll be thinking about you!"

"Well, if you are thinking of me, just how good can your book really be?"

"My book is not your concern. But you might be the face on the other side of it..." she chuckled. I'd had enough of this sexual torment and torture. I hoped my wife wouldn't mind a little turn about. Something told me, she would so I wasn't going to ask.

Now it was my turn to lean in close, then I stepped closer still. Moneypenny looked up at me with her large eyes and a quizzical expression on her face, as I placed my hands on her hips, I brought my face down towards hers and she turned her head slightly to meet me, as though we were going to kiss. But with less than an inch separating our lips, I paused and whispered, "Oh Moneypenny, what man would not give his right arm to be in that position. To be that close to you...to help you with your...with... your reading."

Still whispering, "If it were me, I would find it impossible to keep my hands off of you, I live for the moment when I could help you...*moisturize*. And not just your shaven areas. We mustn't neglect the rest of you..."

I held my hands firmly to her waist as I started to message the skin the beneath her cotton blouse, the small of her back, then around to her sides with my thumbs stretching around to her flat stomach, gradually climbing higher to her ribs. "I would see to it my hands were dripping with lotion, as my calloused hands smoothly glide over that soft naked flesh of yours. I can see you now, with your eyes closed, mouth slightly open, breath coming in short ragged gasps. I'm sure I can feel your diaphragm expand as you inhale deeply." About now my hands were perfectly poised beneath her breasts, right along the bottom side of her heavenly soft swells.

"Then, when my hands make first contact with those fantastic breasts of yours," at this point, I slide my hands up higher, on to her breasts, but so lightly my hands glided over her blouse, I wanted her to wonder if I actually, really touching her or if it was just her imagination. I wanted to leave her skin itching and sensitized. I felt her diaphragm expand sharply as my fingers gently caressed the sides of her breasts and my thumbs so lightly brushed over her nipples. *This alone, was worth the prank.*

Now, I really heard her inhale, so I started again, "Yes, you inhale so deep, expand your chest even more, my guess is that you are trying to push your breasts into my hands harder, but I wont allow it." I could feel her leaning forward into my hands, trying to make the contact with her softness more firm, more certain. However, I was having none of it. I kept my touch, very questionably light.

"Then, as you exhale, my hands glide smoothly down from your breasts, over your stomach and sides then smoothly gliding and smearing the cream over your stomach, and I feel your breath catch in your throat on your exhale, as my fingers are smearing *your cream*...errr ah...moisturizer over your mons, sliding over but feeling the contours of your slit, just the lightest touch over the little hooded bandito down there..." I did feel her breath catch in her throat, but I continued, "sliding and gliding down to your belly, and then...then...to your shaven area. Where I slather it with cream..." I felt her hand at my shoulder pressing more firmly. I paid it no heed. I pulled our pelvises together and I wrapped one arm behind her back to pull her perfect breasts to my chest. They had to be almost a D Cup. Perhaps a C+? Her eyes were now half closed and looked mottled, cloudy and moist, her right hand was on my shoulder, ready to pull me in for a proper kiss. But for that moment, we drank in each other's souls as our breath mingled and mixed. She was almost panting now, her eyes little more than narrow slits. She brought her left arm up around my neck and crossed her hands behind my neck, I felt her begin to tighten and pull me in...

Instead I took both wrists and held her hands to my chest, "Fortunately for me, I have no time. Have a nice day Moneypenny."

I didn't think this conversation was going to be funny anymore if it went on further, so I let her go and turned my attention back to Tommy who had just gotten off of the phone. "We can fly Molson Air back to Mehtar Lam Tuesday at 19:00."

"Sounds good."

We turned and left. She was still standing there a full thirty seconds later, hands still open and empty in front of her at waist high. Her eyes still narrow, mouth still half open, I'd like to think that I saw her knees quiver, but honestly speaking, that may have been wishful thinking.

Before I turned the last corner, "Rick," she called out. I stopped and turned to see her still transfixed. Then I saw her eyes, even at this distance I saw it, they went slowly to a rage. *Ha! Got her!*

Then after a few seconds, her eyes softened and her smile returned, "Be careful Rick."

"I will," and turned to go.

"Rick!" she almost yelled. I looked, "By God, I mean it. Be careful," she said it slowly as if I were an imbecile.

I gave her a half wave and left. Later, it occurred to me how I had misread that tone and cadence. *Perhaps it was genuine concern? No matter. I ain't gettin' planted here.*

* * * *

13:00

Tommy and I took the pathetically small meager files that we had on the al Qaeda leadership to the Bagram Resident Agency Office of the FBI. My thought was that they have been making hay off of their Behavior Science Unit for years. Now I wanted to put it to the test in a different arena.

We turned over what files we had on the personalities in play, and asked for a real quick generic forensics psychological workup on what we had. The Agent must've been super bored because she said, "Sure, I'll give 'em a read right now and type up a couple of paragraphs on each. Where do I find you guys at?"

"More than likely, we'll either be at the CJSOTF J-2 section or we'll be hiding in the transient quarters at Camp Montrond. You can call us on our cell numbers inside the first file on a yellow sticky."

"I'm Special Agent Liz Thompson, so you'll definitely be hearing from me. Probably tomorrow morning."

"Gee, I really didn't expect you to put a rush on it, but I sure am grateful. I don't normally get this kind of cooperation from the bureau."

"All they have me doing here is simple background checks and investigations. However, since none of the country was computerized before we got here, and there was no central record keeping to speak of, they're no records to check. No birth certificates. No county sheriff's office. No court house. Nothing. Most of these people don't even know what their birthdates are, for Christ's sake."

Tommy piped in, "You don't have to tell us. We know exactly how things are here. I'm Special Agent Tom Allen."

"Trust me Liz, there's *nothing* special about him," I jeered, throwing a thumb at Tommy.

"I'll be thrilled to do something law enforcement related again," said Liz.

"You've got experience in this sort of work?" I asked.

"I've never been assigned to the BAU, as they're calling it now Behavioral Analysis Unit, but I have had a number of courses on the subject and eager to give it a try."

"Just give us your best guess where you think we might be able to give them a poke and see a bulge."

"You guys got it. Thanks for coming by." Her smile was gleamed all toothy white, she was practically beaming. That white smile stood in such contrast to her deep dark tan. Being the pig that I am, I wondered where she lay out at. *No! I shook my head clear of the thought. Back to business. It's clear, she had been doing quite a bit of tanning since her arrival.* This made me aware of my perpetual milky/pasty white complexion. Oh well, no tanning time for the weary.

While we walked back to the CJSOTF I had to harass Tommy, "Hey Liz, I'm a Special Agent too! I'm part of your same cool club."

"Hey that's what my title is."

"Oh, I know it. I also know that it doesn't carry any weight in our shop, or in my arena. Nobody's impressed. Now of course, I'm sure that the extremely pleasant shape of Special Agent Thompson had nothing to do with your slinging the Agent title out there."

"She is rather easy on the eyes."

"I'll bet you guys start calling each other Agent Thompson and Agent Allen, like you're on the *X-Files* or something."

"Well, that would be proper..." he rolled his eyes at the thought, because he knew despite it being proper and professional, it would be ridiculous.

* * * *

Tuesday, 11:00
"Hey Rick? Tom? This is Liz Thompson, FBI..."

"Hey Liz, what do you have for us?"

"Well, your files didn't really have a lot to go on. I called back to Quantico yesterday afternoon, and got them just as they were getting into work. I had them pull what we had on these guys and fax me some additional pages. I made copies and beefed up your records a little. I think I was able to put together a pretty comprehensive workup on your panel here. I call it a panel because it seems almost like a Mafia, or organized crime structure to me. One boss with a dozen consigliore's."

"Yeah, that's exactly right, Liz. What I'm hoping to do here is get all of the consigliore's to start feeding on each other like a pack of piranha."

"Okay, let's talk about that over lunch. I'll meet you at Camp Montrond at 12:00?"

"I don't want you to have to walk all the way down here."

"You guys have the best DFAC pronounced; *Dee* Fak= Dining Facility = Mess Hall for us Old Soldiers on Bagram. Trust me, I don't mind."

"Tommy and I will be waiting at the front gate for you."

* * * *

12:10

It is a simple law of physics that women will always keep men waiting. Sometime longer than others, and there seems to be no reasonable formula for this difference. I no longer ask why. I just accept it. Liz walked through the gate and displayed her FBI Operations Center OPCEN Pass to the guard on duty. She shifted her brief case in order to shake hands with us and we steered her towards the utopia she so desperately sought. Our Mess hall.

Yeah, really. We did.

We put together a few trays and found a table. We kept our voices low and sat huddled together in order to be heard over the din.

"I think you have a very interesting situation. You have so many people with the same massive ego complexes that it's a wonder that they are even capable of functioning at all. Most of these guys are really border-megalomaniacs. There's a few here that might be a little more pliable. The one you recruited over the weekend, looks like he is a good source to have. Pretty passive aggressive, will be more than happy to give everybody enough rope to hand themselves with, and then step in as the heir' apparent while all of the bodies are still swinging from the trees. He's the perfect 'button man,' this is a term used to describe the individual who pushes "buttons" to make the machine move = agent provocateur.

"Okay, the leader of Taliban activities in the northeast is Kwami Maqbid, which one of these underlings is most ripe for the plucking, in your eyes?" I asked.

"Well he has a number of lieutenants that are really close trusted associates. Any of them would hurt terribly, but they don't really command any soldiers or fighters. They are more or less in enforcer roles. Your files show that Jamal Illand*allah* has the largest army of some five thousand fighters, so right off the top I would say his absence or betrayal would probably hurt the worse. Plus, he's a spoiled rotten little rich kid who is only used to having things his way and no other way. If something terrible happens, you can be sure, he'll be looking to point a finger or throw somebody else out in front of him to be the sacrificial lamb."

"Yeah, I read that file too, and came to the same conclusion but just for the numbers aspect alone. While I strongly doubt he could ever muster five thousand troops in the field, his influence and ability to recruit would be a hard blow to absorber."

"How large do you think his army is?"

"I'd be surprised if he could put a full thousand in the field; probably eight hundred at most. There's a thing here we call 'Haji Math'. Ten will be reported as a hundred and a hundred as a thousand."

"Yeah, I'm familiar with it. So you think his numbers are padded? Based on what?"

"Just my best guess. Which of the other commanders do you think would be the best patsy?"

"I've given that some considerable thought, and I think this one..." she said as she handed me a file. Clearly she was trying to adhere to the OPSEC Operational Security rules. Don't discuss people, places, dates or times in any public venue. I respected that.

I was looking at the file of Ishmaeli Abdullah. I smiled because I liked her choice. "This is a shit head we were playing games with back in 2003. I handed the file to Tommy who instantly started nodding his head 'yes'.

"I'd love to put him in a jam," Tommy said.

"Okay, Liz. Thank you so much! We are going to fly back tonight, and we'll try and set up a meeting with our source for later in the week, then we'll try to put something together. This is some outstanding work you did here, and we won't forget it. If there's anything we can do for you in return, just call us. Seriously."

"Actually, I wanted to talk to you guys about that."

I smiled because I half expected it. She wanted to go out into the field with us. She leaned in even closer and practically whispered it, "Can I go out with you guys sometime? I hate being stuck here in Bagram. If I was DEA, I'd be out in the bush all the time, but the FBI? Here?"

Tommy and I looked at each other, and I knew that he wouldn't mind, being a 'not-so-Special Agent' and all that silly horse shit. Tommy was non-committal which is his MO *Modus Operandi*. Never stick your neck out. Let somebody else make the decisions.

When he didn't say anything, I told her, "Liz, if anything comes up, you're going to be the first call I make. It may not be what you want it to be, but it will get you out of the office. That's all I can promise at this point."

Her smile went from ear to ear, and she was really as giddy as a school girl. In fact, I had no idea just how giddy a school girl was, until that moment.

"Oh, thank you so much! It'll mean the world to me. I won't get in anybody's way. I'll do exactly what I am told to do. You won't have a bit of trouble out of me," she said to reaffirm our decision.

Hell, it was my decision! If something went wrong with this, I knew Tommy would throw me under the bus with both hands, "I never thought it was a good idea," he'd say.

"I know you will. We have your number. I don't know when, but you will be hearing from us. How easily do you travel?"

"I can be anywhere overnight, if I have to. The bureau keeps a chopper here for us permanently; I can have the pilot here in a half hour."

Tommy finally spoke up, "You should know, it can get pretty hairy out there."

I couldn't let that slide, "As if you would know, Tommy!" I rolled my eyes and shook my head.

"Don't listen to this oaf!" He said, jabbing a thumb in my direction. "Do you have the proper 'accessories' for this sort of thing?"

"Well, I have a 9mm Colt Submachine gun, and of course my pistol. I was hoping that if I needed anything more than that, you would be able to get it for me."

"Just like in civilian life. Wardrobe is all about the accessories. And yeah, we can get you anything else, if you need it," I said. "I just want to make you aware, it's not all fun and games out there."

With that, she did a small silent clapping of her hands, grinning like the cat that ate ten canaries. "No, it isn't. I know that. But I'd be happy to do anything I can to help you guys out."

In the Intelligence business, there are many fields. Such as: Human Intelligence HUMINT, Signals Intelligence SIGINT, Imagery Intelligence, IMINT, etc. These are called disciplines. My idea was a rather simple inexpensive deception plan that all hinged on word of mouth with some supplemental documents. This is something that I like to call BOGINT; Bogus Intelligence or RUMINT; Rumor Intelligence.

"Okay, now I think this is critical. The best thing about propaganda is, is that it doesn't have to be true. You, me, everybody needs to start talking about how much of the Taliban leadership that we have been able to co-opt and leave in place. Whenever we are at a bazaar, or in a restaurant, a café, whenever we are around the local nationals, we talk about all the leadership that we now have on the payroll. Sooner or later, it's going to get back to them and then they won't know who to trust. When that happens, they'll start to feed on each other. Maybe in a couple of month's time, we leak a story to the press tailoring it down to one or two problem children. Hopefully, we can get them to do our dirty work for us."

"What about your agents?"

Say Good Night

"That brings up the second facet of our plan. I held up a folder that was clearly and boldly Ricked Top Secret—No Foreignn Disemination—Noforn. Tommy and I both typed up reports detailing our efforts to capture Marid Law Watiri, and how they became a dismal failure. Despite our best efforts he made a bold, brilliant and daring escape with four other unidentified operatives. This should bolster his credibility a little. We want to be careful though, because 'thou doth protest too loudly'. Right after we leave here, we are going over to the Green Beans at the PX and have us some coffee, then conveniently forget this there for about thirty minutes." In addition to the reports we had typed up, I had it stuffed with all sorts of rudimentary paperwork and simple military forms. If I do say so myself, it was a pretty convincing piece of bait.

"There's a great idea."

"Yeah, it's not bad. But it's a hand we can over-play. We can only do this once or twice. My bet is by the third time, they would probably get wise to us."

"After we loose these documents? Do we just walk away?"

"Then we are going to come back looking for it, fake incredulity that we lost it, have the MP's come and lock the place down while we search for the file. After all, if it was really Top Secret material, we would move mountains to try and get it back. So, we have to put on a show. Can I buy you a cup of coffee?"

"I was just thinking I'd like a latte."

"But back to your agent. We'll let him be?"

"We'll keep him covered and out of suspicion. For as long as we can anyways. He's not upper management so he won't fall under their microscope for quite awhile."

With that she stood up, grabbed her tray and in a clear audible tone of voice said, "Rick that was quite a coup landing the number one and two Taliban warlords. Getting them on the payroll is really going to make a difference."

A clever girl. She knows that being as pretty as she is, her mere presence already had two hundred eyes on her, and that GI's are the worse for loose talk, and that they would now go to the PX, to the bazaar, to the local nationals shops and all start talking about what they heard in the mess hall from that "really hot FBI agent".

"Yeah, I'm pretty pleased. But we still have to see what he's willing to give up," I said in response. The seeds were planted.

By 13:30 we were working on our second round of coffee. Liz had a Mocha Latte, Tommy a Chai Latte and me my traditional double shot of espresso. War is hell. That's why I refuse to go to the Dairy Queen outside. And only once, by force of coercion did I eventually try the Pizza Hut. It wasn't bad. By 14:00, we stood and walked out and meandered through the PX for thirty minutes. I had left the file partially covered, but clearly visible under a copy of *Stars and Stripes*.

We really didn't know that there was an enemy sympathizer working at the PX or Green Beans. We just sort of assumed it.

We went back. The file was gone. Looking frantic and perplexed, we asked all of the employees if anybody had seen it. Everybody denied any knowledge. We made a 'frantic' search of the interior, and then a search of all of the garbage cans and bags outside. We found the almost entirely empty folder there, in a garbage bag. Missing were the two reports that Tommy and I had typed up detailing our efforts to capture Law Watiri.

We then called the MP's and made a thorough search of the premises and garbage. Since Tommy was a Counterintelligence Agent, I allowed him to give me, 'the dressing down of my life'. Liz also got into the act and read me my Miranda Rights even though they don't apply in Military cases, it was all for show, after being questioned by the two of them for an hour in the Green Beans sitting area, she handcuffed me and she and Tommy both drove me back to the CJSOTF.

* * * *

Tuesday, 15:00

I'd looked for Moneypenny in J-2 shop, but was told that she'd taken the afternoon off. So now I found myself walking to her quarters, a dangerous position for a married man like myself to be in. Especially when talking about a carnivore like Moneypenny!

She stayed in a collection of Conex shipping containers that were split up into small apartments then stacked on top of one another in two, sometimes three stories. These were what we referred to as, 'Man Cans'. They made for a relatively comfortable existence, given the circumstances. Hers was a few hundred yards off of Disney Drive in Bagram. Disney Drive was named for a soldier who died on the first iteration here, resulting from a tragic welding accident. I knocked on her door and got no answer. However, I knew that she like to tan herself on the roof of the building to keep that fantastic body of hers out from under prying eyes. Most women here did. So, up to the roof I went. *Into the belly of the beast!*

She was the only one on the roof, her red, white and blue, Union Jack bikini was unmistakable. As I approached, "Moneypenny. Well, here you are."

She sat up and held her hand over her eyes to see me in the sun. "Well, Richard. This is a very pleasant surprise. You are just in time."

"Just in time for what?" I asked.

"To rub some lotion on my back, it's time for me to turn over," she said holding a bottle of sun-tan lotion.

I took the bottle from her, knowing that it was her, who was raising the ante now. Well, I've never been one to back down from a dare. I took the bottle and filled my hands with the lotion, then knelt beside her as she rolled over, ever so slowly to give me such a feasting look at her bounty. My God... As she got herself situated on her stomach, positioned her breasts, so they were comfortable, she reached back and untied the knot holding her bikini top closed at both her neck and her back. Then she pulled her hair out of the way and explained, "I hate bikini lines."

"Me too," I said, with hands dripping of lotion.

"So, to what do I owe this unexpected, but very pleasant visit?"

"I just came by to say 'Good bye,' the Brigadier is sending me back to Mehtar Lam. I suppose I'm doing penance, for loosing a file."

With her face turned toward me and her eyes closed, she nodded, "Yes, I heard about that before I left work. All the 'weenies' as you like to say were so jubilant that you, the might American Military Intelligence, Special Forces falls flat on his face. I didn't say a word. I just knew it didn't sound at all like you. I know better."

Wanting to keep the security of the operation in tact, "Well, it's the sort of thing that can happen to anybody. I feel like a goof for such a stupid mistake. There might be some hell to pay for this. It's the sort of thing that could ruin my career."

Moneypenny was unimpressed. I don't think I'll worry about that. After all, these sort of things happen all the time." This told me that while she was not specifically 'read-in' on the operation, she had a fair idea of what was going on. After all, she did work for MI-6.

My wife and I had ordered and studied a series of message videos some years back, and I now tried to apply the Cliff notes from those, as my hands pressed into the very near nakedness of Moneypenny, and glided over her flesh. Smoothly my hands flowed over that flawless skin of hers. I'd started at her neck, messaging the tight muscles there, worked down over the tops of her shoulders, then her upper back, shoulder blades and the center of her back, she moaned so provocatively. I was stoic. Unfazed. I was thinking that if my wife could see me now, I'd be certainly buried in the back yard, in a shallow grave. *Oh well. I promise Kathie, I won't go too far...* More lotion. Much more lotion.

Before moving to the middle of her back, I allowed myself the opportunity to apply more lotion to her sides, from her arm pits down to her waist, allowing myself a generous feel of the sides of those fantastic breasts, as their copious softness bulged out from her sides. Now, it was her turn to be stoic. More lotion.

As I moved down to her middle back, she moaned again, even louder, "This is quite a bit more than smearing lotion. You should do this professionally."

"No I shouldn't. I shouldn't do it to you, either."

"Ahhh, but here you are..."

"Well, I'm never one to leave a friend in a lurch."

"Well, thank you for that, ohhhh...ohhh...uhhhh..."

I began to work on her lower back and waist. I was rewarded with the sounds of Moneypenny in near ecstasy. There could be no doubt, that I was in fact, the luckiest man in Afghanistan at this point. Every heterosexual male in country wished they could be me at this minute. When I was faced with the prospect of messaging her rump, I decided to shift gears. But not without raising the ante again. I untied the two bows at her hips, which held her bikini bottom in place and then folded the back flap down away from her 'arse' as they like to say. I feasted my eyes on the exquisite site of Moneypenny's bare bum. As I expected, there was not a hair in sight.

"I think I'll do your legs now."

Moneypenny offered no resistance. I started at the tops of her thighs, I made sure to get the crease between the bottom of her marvelous ass and the tops of her thighs, I paid particular attention to her inner thighs, getting all the way up to the crease in between her lower lips and her thighs. More lotion. Her legs parted, granting me access and her ass rose up off of the chaise an inch or so, and whether it was perspiration or something else, there was an obvious dampness coming from her center.

I focused on the backs of her legs and knees on my way down to her ankles. On the way back up, I would focus on her inner legs. Down to the backs of her knees. Down to her calves. Then lastly her ankles. Then, I was much quicker moving back up to her thighs. Especially, her inner thighs. I slathered her bare flesh with so much oil, it splashed slightly as my hands made contact with her skin. She was moaning and breathing hard. She turned her face away from me now.

I worked more lotion into her bare bum, my palms and finger free, smoothly roamed over fleshy globes and firmly messaged the pillow softness there. I contemplated working some into the crack of her ass, but knew that was going too far. Her ass raised up to meet my hands another two inches and I knew, this was my moment.

I acted surprise, "Oh my gosh, look at the time. Take care, Moneypenny. I'll see you when I get back into town." With that, I stood up, and made for the ladder.

"Richard! Wait!"

"Sorry, I've got to go. I have a flight to catch." I saw her make a horrible face.

"Damn it! Oh Shit! Uuuggghhh! Oh Shit! Just...just...just be careful... Goddamn You!" She pounded the chaise she lay on in clear and obvious frustration.

You are a pig Richard! I'm ashamed of you...but, very few men would've even tried to stop especially given as far as you got. I argued with myself. *You have a wife who won't take kindly to this sort of conduct... No matter. It's over. Round two of Sexual Frustrating Master of the Universe, goes to me! No, maybe not. You're in as bad a condition as she is, you idiot!*

* * * *

23:45
Finally back in Mehtar Lam. Calling it a night.

* * * *

Wednesday, 10:30
We made contact with our agent, Marid and arranged to meet for coffee at a shop in J-Bad we new and liked, and also wasn't far from his place. He told he could be there within twenty minutes of our call. So, we met him at 11:00 promptly.

He took the table next to ours where we could talk and be heard in the relative quiet of the café, but still not have to be at the same table.

We asked him some detailed questions about Jamal Illand*allah* and he said that "Jamal plans next week to go to Pakistan and bring in two thousand new recruits from there. With the latest unrest in northeast Pakistan, there were internment camps scattered all over the region for Internal Displaced Persons IDPs. These camps have long been a fertile recruiting ground for organizations like Al Qaeda, the Hezbollah Islamic Gullebudin HIG, etc. Everybody was aware of the unrest in the Swat Valley, near the Khyber Pass so this made perfect sense, and was a very good litmus test to see just how good the information was going to be from Marid. We pressed him for more details, dates and routes, but he denied any knowledge, yet. He said that he would certainly have more on Sunday, after their counsel meeting.

We made a date for Sunday, same time at a different coffee shop in town.

We made our report to the J-2 staff and left them to decide how they wanted to handle it. Tommy and I were now relegated to our own devices, for the time being.

* * * *

13:10

Just to keep both Moneypenny and the Brigadier informed and up to date, I called Bagram and was mildly surprised when Moneypenny answered the phone, "Hey Moneypenny, it's Richard Burns, how are you today?"

I was afraid that she would be pretty pissed with me, given the context of our last meeting. But Moneypenny didn't miss a beat, "Throbbing, my dear Richard. Just throbbing." She was a consummate professional, she wasn't going to let me see her bleed. Good girl! My respect for her just went up twenty-five points.

"Well, that's very special for you. Could you please plug me into the Brigadier?" I made sure that I spoke firm, steady, with authority. I wasn't bashful, sheepishly or giggling and my voice didn't crack. I had no time for her games or any belly aching. Although I did feel a warm glow of satisfaction at hearing her admission.

Chapter Five

Week ending 8/22/09
Sunday, 16 August 2009. 13:00

It was a bright and sunny day with hardly a cloud in the sky. This means we were approaching the peak heat hours. A good time to get out of the sun.

"Do you feel like some refreshment Tommy?"

"Sure. How about a nice steaming cup of hot coffee?"

"Perfect. What else would you drink on a scorching hot afternoon?"

"I can't think of a thing."

Tommy and I were sitting Kitty corner from the coffee house that Marid had said to meet him at, for the past three hours. We wanted to get eyes on the place and watch to see who came and who left. And more importantly, who stayed.

Over the course of the three hours nobody stayed excessively long. None of the people we kept records on entered the establishment. We waited until our appointment arrived before I went in. He didn't arrive with anybody and he wasn't talking on the phone to anybody when he got there. Tommy stayed outside to cover the street.

I walked inside and took a quick inventory of who was sitting where. Once again, Marid had taken a table in the center of the café, away from any windows, with an open table next to it. I placed my order, took my drink, grabbed a Pashto language paper off of the counter and took my cup to the table beside him. We didn't look at each other, we both fainted to be reading our respective papers. We spoke in very soft barely audible tones.

"Jamal is going to Pakistan tomorrow. He swears he will bring back two thousand new fighters. I think he will come back to Afghanistan on Wednesday so that these fighters will be in place for the election on Thursday."

"Do you know anything about which camp he will collect them from, or which route he will be taking to come into Afghanistan?"

"Not this time. However, I have drawn a map of a route that he has used in the past. Most of the fighters he will not get from one

IDP camp. He will probably get them from four or five camps. He has special recruiters at these camps now. All the details I have on his last recruiting excursions are outlined on a piece of paper inside this newspaper."

Without ever looking at each other, I said, "Put your paper on the edge of the table then take a sip of your drink while you jot a note in your day planner and I'll trade papers with you." He did exactly as he was told and about four seconds later I did the same, laying my newspaper right next to his, while I lit a cigarette, checked the time and took another sip of espresso. Then I picked up his newspaper and pretended to keep reading.

Speaking softly again, "Pick up my paper. Take it with you. Inside is an envelope with 10,000 Afghani about $200.00. You're going to invite as much leadership as you can to your house for dinner and an evening of conversation. We'll wire up your house later. Inside is a second envelope with 15,000 Afghani. This is yours. If this information you've given us is good, there will be more in it for you. You have to trust me."

"I do." Then he finished his tea, grabbed my newspaper and stood to leave. As he side stepped by my table I heard him whisper, *"Salam Al Lekim."*

I whispered back, *"Salam."*

I waited three or four minutes to see if somebody followed him, then I took his newspaper and left.

Next was to type up the Contact Report and call the Brigadier.

* * * *

Monday, 17 August 2009
09:00
"Well, if it is their plan to put two thousand terrorists in our patch, I think that we should have something to say about that. I'll sit down with the J-3 *Operations-Not to be confused with Intelligence Operations, which is a sub-sect of the J-2,* and we'll work up a tasking. Probably a team from your company in J-Bad."

This was easy. "Yes, Sir. We'll talk later."

* * * *

11:30
"Okay, we are on for an Ambush with an ODA a twelve man Operational Detachment-Alpha, the basic Special Forces element,

from your company. You'll report back to your company this afternoon and begin planning and preparations. I don't know which team is going, but at least you'll be with your old Chicago crew."

"Thank you, Sir."

* * * *

14:00

Chief Warrant Officer two, Eric "Grumps" Krampf, was a friend of mine from my first tour over here in 2003. Being a former enlisted swine, he was quite a bit older than most of the men on his team. His German name sounds close enough to Grumps, which they thought, either rightly or wrongly, seemed to fit his persona. Personally I liked the guy. He was a Martial Arts instructor in Kansas City and an ogre of a man. Eric

"Look, I've given you everything he gave me. You've got everything I've got."

Eric said, "I've worked with Rick before. If he says that's all he's got, that's all he's got. In this case, I suspect that's all there is."

"You're better not be holding out on us. Because I'm telling you, this intelligence is incomplete," he said shaking his head in suspicious frustration. I was empathetic, but I was loosing patience.

I put a look on my face, "Look Captain, that's the nature of intelligence. It's always incomplete. All we can give is our best read on it. At the end of the day, it boils down to: Would you rather live with the consequences of your *actions*? Or the consequences of your *inactions*?"

This seemed to soften his resistance, a little. The Team Commander, CPT Ryan Holstein was typical in this regard. Most teams are always pretty suspicious of any Intelligence missions that get tasked to them. They are afraid of being left out on a limb, or because the Intelligence side, didn't come clean with all of the information, that they'll all wined up getting killed because of that key piece of information we didn't release. It's not without some justification. The intelligence side of the house was not at all forthcoming during Vietnam.

"How good do you think these numbers are?"

"Two thousand? I would be very suspicious of that. Generally, I'd say we might see two hundred. This guy has a history of delivering big numbers. I'd say we better plan to see two thousand, but don't be surprised if it's five hundred or so."

"Five hundred could give us a pretty thorough ass kicking."

While a full strength ODA is normally twelve men, this ODA was under strength, by one Junior Communications Commo Sergeant, one Junior Medic, and one Operations and Intelligence Sergeant. Being Intelligence with a strong communications background, I could fill one of those posts and be an alternate for a second. This brought the team's number from nine to ten. Everybody had to be trained in two specialties.

"I'm aware. But the up side there is; if they were just recruited, they can't possibly have much in the way of training. These sound like disposable triggermen being sent out to be machine-gun fodder on Election Day."

"Well, you'd better hope your right because you are coming with us. This way, no matter what happens, you'll be a victim to your own intelligence."

"How poetic."

* * * *

Tuesday, 18 August 2009
22:00

We inserted into the border region by chopper. A short fifteen minute ride and we were on the ground moving again. He had a series of remote electronic sensors that we had to emplace along certain trails that crossed the border. Ideally, we wanted all of these sensors in place well before sun rise. By 22;50, we had established out Patrol Base from which we would conduct operations.

I was fairly certain that we were not going to see a parade of two thousand Taliban come down a single trail, lined up nice for us like ducks in a shooting gallery. Be that as it may, we were all carrying a double basic load of ammunition a basic load being 210 rounds of 5.56mm, and fourty-five rounds of 9mm, but because of the potential numbers everybody was carrying twice their normal load. I thought they would probably come across on numerous trails and join up on this side of the border. According to the details provided to me by Marid, he stated that a mosque in the center of Dowgar was a frequent assembly area for Jamal. That's where I had my chips for the assembly this time.

The sensor that I had to emplace was six klicks from our patrol base. I left out to put it in place at 23:38. While moving to our Patrol Base, the moon was high and bright. It made movement easy. There were belts and belts of stars in the sky that were so bright and you saw so far, with a little more imagination, one might feel as though he were a part of the milky way and not just a spectator.

Now, at almost midnight, the moon was still high, but it wouldn't stay there. I wanted to get to my point and get my sensor in the ground before I lost it completely. With the added assistance of my night vision goggles, NVGs, I moved easily and quickly through the moonlight. At least as easily and quickly as anybody could going over such mountainous terrain. I found my trail and moved along it for a few hundred meters toward Pakistan, looking for a good location. When I found one, I scraped out a real quick hole, placed the sensor in, then poured water over the top of it so there would be no loose soil surrounding it, that it feel every tiny tremor and vibration. Surprisingly, I was back at the Patrol Base by 01:52.

* * * *

Wednesday, 19 August 2009
02:00
My watch. Mind numbing boredom on top of a grueling walk in from the chopper. The distance wasn't so great, but we were heavy with ammunition and radio batteries, and the worse of all, body armor. Nearly forty pounds of armor on top of everything else. Still, a mild but highly stressful walk to emplace my device, followed by the most boring sixty minutes of your life. It can be almost impossible to stay awake. However, at the same time, on the eve of battle not trying to sound melodramatic, nobody really sleeps. After my watch, I slipped into that very light sort of sleep some call alpha sleep—where you are constantly aware of everything going on around you, but not really quite awake. It's not at all restful.

Through your mind swirl all sorts of worries and concerns. What if this... What if that... The possibilities and worries were endless.

* * * *

05:00
At some point I must've fallen asleep because Eric woke me with a cup of coffee. "Wake up Grandpa," he teased.

He always gave me crud about that, even though he was a good four years older than me. As I sat up, my neck was stiff and hurt, my ears hurt from using my body armor as a pillow. My back hurt from sleeping on the ground. My legs were stiff and hurt... I really just hurt everywhere. I was too old for this sort of stuff ten years ago!

I took the canteen cup Eric offered me, "God Bless you, Eric."

"Let's just hope he continues to."

"Yes, let's hope."

We were all awake and at the ready. This is called 'stand to,' where everybody is on a hundred percent alert, ready for an attack, one hour before sunrise until one hour after sunrise. Then the normal sleep schedule can go back in affect.

Some people had much greater distances to cover than I did last night, but all of them found their trails and planted their sensors, and made it back well before sunrise. The last team making it in by 04:00.

We left one man awake all night, and we alternated who it was. This way, not everybody would be trying to sleep in the peak 140 degree heat of the day. Impossible. Sleep on operations is always very fleeting. Sometimes a downright impossibility.

* * * *

10:39

The first sensors started showing a greatly increased volume of foot traffic. Within a few minutes, another started showing rather light but, near continuous light truck traffic. Gradually, all of the sensors started reporting in. Then they continued to report in. Then they continued, and continued and finally, continued.

It was starting to look as though their prophecy of two thousand Al Qaeda was coming to fruition. In which case, the ten of us might be in for some very interesting times. "We're gonna moved down and get eyes on that mosque and hope that that's his rally point again. In the mean time, we better get our artillery support on the phone and tell them to warm up those pre-plotted targets," CPT Holstein said.

I grabbed the handset for the Satellite Communications Radio SATCOM and gave the "gun-bunnies" in our Artillery a heads up that we may be calling soon for an express delivery. Then I called the OPCEN and told them that we had some preliminary indications a high volume of concentrated traffic along all monitored crossing points. The hair on the back of my neck stood up, because I may truly have bit off more than I can chew.

* * * *

11:45
Crowds began forming in the small square in front of the mosque. We kept a count as the crowd grew. By noon, the crowd was over two hundred people, and every single one of them was armed. Not with bolt action Enfield Rifles, with brand-new Russian AK-47's. Gradually over the next three hours, as crowds drifted in from their various trails and paths, the crowd began to swell, filling the town square to overflow. We estimated now that they had a crowd of eight hundred.

Ryan crawled over to my location and said, "Rick, you struck gold this time. You have good Mojo. Let's give them another hour or so, just to see how big this crowd gets. However, if our Boy Jamal shows up, all bets are off. I'm gonna start dropping red hot steel on their heads."

"Roger, Sir. All the same, I'm gonna start getting some air assets lined up."

"Good idea." He gave me a pat on the shoulder and crawled back to his vantage point.

"Tango two seven, tango two seven, this is November niner-niner, over…" Tango two seven was a squadron of Apache Attack Helicopters that carry 20mm chain linked machine guns that spit thousands of round a minute, and usually 57mm rocket pods and racks that carry a virtual cornucopia of death. The destruction that can be wrought by these birds would impress, even Satan himself. This squadron was assigned to directly support us on this operation.

A distant voice on the radio responded, "November niner-niner, this is Tango two seven, how does your party look down there?"

"Attendance is fantastic! We may need some assistance in keeping this crowd entertained."

"I'm just coming from another party, but I still have a little ordinance left. Whatever I got, you are welcome to it."

"I'm afraid we can't use your special talents yet. We want to see if there are any late arrivals, perhaps a surprise guest."

"How much time are you guys willing to give me?"

"You've got at the very least an hour. Odds are we are going to hit them with Artillery first."

"You just let me know. I never miss one of your parties!"

"Thanks, the invitation is perpetual."

* * * *

13:00

I felt that vice cranking down on my head again. Always. Every time, right before combat. It's worse when you can see it coming. When it's a surprise, the tension doesn't have enough time to build.

The crowd had now swollen to well over a thousand Al Qaeda and there were still small groups trickling in. We decided to give it a little more time, when at 13:20, an individual that looked remarkably like Jamal took to the steps of the mosque and raised his hands for quiet. He had crossed bandoliers, a` la Pancho Villa, with Russian palm Z-5 hand grenades hanging as though they were ornaments. I looked through my 25X Bushnell spotter's scope and confirmed that was indeed the individual known to us as Jamal. Now that we had PID Positive Identification, we were cleared to fire at any time. He was 1100 meters away. I could get him with a rifle shot, but that really isn't what we wanted. We wanted him disgraced as a potential traitor, as a man who recruited 2,000 new terrorists and then offered them up to the Coalition as a present. This whole thing worked best if he lived.

When the Osama bin Laden posters came out, it made our blood boil. This was followed with their cries, *"Allah aq Baaarrrrh!"*

I had not heard Tango 27 come back up on the air yet, so Ryan took the FM radio Handset from the other commo man and spoke into it, "Bravo sixty-three, Bravo sixty-three, this is November ninety-one, over..."

"November Niner one, go ahead..."

"I got more bad guys down here than ants at a company picnic. No shit, I got at least a thousand, maybe twelve hundred! I need for you guys to fire, Pre-plot target number one, let me have the first couple of rounds to adjust, make them HE he mentioned that as though it were an after-thought, 'Oh yeah, make that HE would you please? HE meaning High Explosive. I got that target at a little over a thousand meters, on an azimuth of 265 magnetic."

"Roger November niner one, copy you to fire Pre-plot number one at a distance of 1000 meters, 265 magnetic, and you have troops in the open. Is that correct?"

"Roger Bravo sixty-three."

"Roger, Stand by."

After about two minutes later, "November niner one, shot,

over..." They had just pulled the lanyard on the big 155mm howitzer.

"Shot, out." He acknowledged their fire.

"November niner one, splash, over..." The round now had five seconds to impact.

"Splash, out." Ryan responded.

I heard the round fly overhead and everybody looked up. Then, total silence.

Just before the ear shattering ka rumph! We saw a large cloud of black and gray smoke appear just on the far edge of town from us. Ryan was excited, "Bravo six three, shift right two hundred and fire for effect! Let's make this a Battery six meaning; firing all six guns in the Battery and hit 'em with some Willy Peter!"

"Roger, November niner one. Firing Battery six, Willy Pete." Willy Pete is a military slang term for White Prosperous, an incendiary which burns at temperatures that hell can even reach. He wanted to burn that square to the ground with as many people as he could get.

"Shot, over..."

"Shot, out." Five seconds to impact.

The crowd looked at the column of smoke from the previous round, while a few smart ones started to make a break for cover. Ninety percent of the Sheeple a slang hybrid for sheep/people, were quite content to stand still for their impeding death. Once again. Totally silent in those five seconds, and they seemed to go on forever.

This mosque and square was located in a collection of mud huts that may have once been a town, of sorts. It was likely abandoned since the Soviet occupation. There was no standing population to worry about.

The first cluster of six rounds all impacted on the edge of the square and tall clouds of white smoke and white glowing embers showered out in every direction. The pandemonium in the square was like nothing I had ever seen before. It was littered and layered in dead and dying, or worse, alive and burning.

The surrounding mud huts afforded good shelter for some and the smart ones started to pile inside those. The smartest ones, began to flee altogether and never looked back. Ryan's adjustment was a little off to one side of the square and therefore didn't land dead center. It sure had the desired effect.

I was looking through my spotter's scope and could no longer see Jamal. I grabbed my binos and scanned the crowd for him.

I heard Ryan on the radio again, "Bravo six three, shift left five-zero and fire for effect, again."

I shook my head again at Ryan and Eric's daring and glaring incompetence! They had decided to share the same fox hole. The only two officers on the team would be situated in the same position. They said it was because they wanted to centralize communications assets. The reality was it was Ryan's youth and immortality and Eric's denial to the possibility that he really actually might get killed. Oh well, I'm not in charge...

"Roger, left five zero and fire for effect, Battery six, again, Willy Pete."

"Roger, Willy Pete."

"Shot, over."

"Shot, out."

"Splash, over."

"Splash, out."

This time, the second series of six rounds did land dead center of the square, however, since most people had cleared out there for the relative cover of the surrounding mud huts, it did not have quite the same impact as the first.

Then over the SATCOM, "November niner-niner, this is Tango two seven, what's your status, over?"

Ryan heard this and quickly spoke into the FM handset, "Bravo six three, check fire, check fire Bravo six three, we have aviation assets in the area. I need for you to remain in a cold status until further, over.

"Roger, November niner one. Going cold, we'll be on standby."

Ryan came and took the SATCOM handset from me, and said, "Tango two seven, we are glad to have you back, this is November niner one."

"Sorry November niner one, it took me a little longer than I had thought. I decided to top off on fuel while I was down, so I can give you the maximum coverage time."

"Trust me, I'm grateful for it. I hit them with some artillery and it would seem most of the smarter ones are holed up inside the mud huts. Do you think you guys could make a pass?"

"We'd love to." With that, their blades leapt forward from the distance. I looked to the west and saw seven Apaches, their rocket pods clearly visible, as they steered in our general direction.

"I'm going to be moving my team down into their ambush positions now, so don't take on any movement you might see on the hill side," Ryan said.

"Roger," came the short simple reply.

The choppers swooped down the hillside and let rip with their machine guns. A solid orange rope of tracers came from the barrels of every Apache as they hosed down the streets and whatever nooks and crannies they could see of any mud hut. Now for every orange round that you see fired from these guns, had five more additional rounds right behind that you CAN'T see! When no legitimate targets were in view, they chewed away at the walls of the mud huts, taking their precious cover.

In the meantime on the hillside, "Okay everybody, time to ruck-up. We're going to move down to our ambush position and set up the kill zone."

Several RPG Soviet Anti Tank weapons = Rocket Propelled Grenade, could be seen arching up toward the choppers. None hit, thank God.

We all gathered our gear and moved down the 250 meters to our positions. Normally, in an ambush, a couple of men are positioned further out, but at both ends of the majority of the team. These are known as the security teams. Their job is to ensure that nobody enters or leaves the kill zone, once the ambush has been executed. With the enemy spread out over an area several hundred meters in diameter, it was unlikely we were going to get anybody on the far side of our guests. We would use our artillery support to close that door, with a wall of white hot razor blades. They only had two real choices: Run east, toward Pakistan and we would seal that route with Artillery. Or run west, towards the choke point on the road to J-Bad, through the mountain pass, where we were situated on the northern hillside.

This, was by no means, a typical ambush. Even with tremendous air assets, ten men taking on over 1200 hundred, is fraught for disaster. Nobody ever said, "Whoa! Man! We need to get out of here." Or, "We are in for it now. There's no hope of wining this one!" Everybody knew, this was the job they signed on for. They were in it, to win it! Nobody was drafted, and they had all volunteered, multiple times. With that, the rest of us crawled into our positions and strung out Claymore mines these are mines that are about the size of a shoe box lid, loaded with a pound of C-4 explosives and a sheet of steel ball bearings that act as projectiles when the mine is detonated with a handheld clacker, its on folding legs to stick into the ground and aim toward the enemy to our front. We did put one Security team out, to the west of us about fifty meters away from the majority of the team, overlooking a road than ran through a mountain pass, which ran from J-Bad to the border.

Over the next hour, the Apaches continued to work their magic and drastically reduce the number of guests remaining at our party. "November niner one, this is tango two seven."

"Go ahead Tango two seven."

"Look, I'm kind of embarrassed here, having to say this, but apparently, we got a little too trigger happy, and we now have to run back to be refitted and reloaded."

Ryan looked like he wasn't so sure of himself anymore. He looked as though somebody and run over his puppy, backed up and did it again! He was that dejected.

"Hurry back, tango two seven."

"You can bet if it's not us, it'll be somebody like us."

That was not what Ryan wanted to hear, right then. Now, he may not get the same guys.

It was now, 16;30! Where the hell did the afternoon go?

* * * *

16:30

As the remaining crowd picked themselves up out of the rubble, they began forming into pockets of three and four, then five to seven and eventually into packs of ten or greater. Initially, they started to walk back to Pakistan, but Ryan had other ideas.

"Bravo six three, this is November niner-one, air support is now cleared from my area, and I need for you to fire Pre-plot missions five and six. I'll adjust, lets make this one a battery six, also, and lets use HE."

"Roger November ninety-one, air assets gone, fire a battery six in HE at pre-plot five and six, over."

"That's a roger."

"Shot over..."

"Shot out."

Six, 155mm Artillery shells impacted in a small cluster at Pre-plotted Artillery targets number five and six. Five and six were a series of trail junctions that all linked up with the larger, more trafficked foot paths which ran north and east through to Pakistan. Most of these fighters probably decided that they would just return on the trail that they came in on. Not so. We had effectively sealed off any avenues to the north and east.

There were several more casualties from that salvo, but not nearly as many as the initial bloodletting. There flavor for

Pakistan now waning, they shifted direction towards the south. Here, the terrain was far more rugged. Ryan fired a series of pre-plot targets on that side of the mosque and mud hut compounds. Any southbound avenues were effectively now closed.

Eventually, they got the message. That way wasn't safe either. Some of them, perhaps, had to be getting the idea, that since we were adjusting on them that we had to have eyes on them. The smarter ones began scouring the hillsides looking for traces of us.

The only remaining, untested route was to the west. Where we were sitting on the mountainside on the north side of the J-Bad road. I doubt it was any real considered move, because they were now essentially just rats in a maze. Now, they all seemed to be drifting toward the J-Bad road and the mountain pass. Right towards us. While we had done quite a bit of damage to their numbers, they were still almost a thousand strong, while that thousand probably had two or three hundred wounded to care for, they were relatively minor or at least not life threatening wounds.

Slowly, they began to close that one thousand meters that initially separated us. They had also formed up into something roughly resembling military units. They assumed rudimentary formations and columns, they carried their weapons at the ready, they moved cautiously, deliberately, with purpose and they were scanning the mountain side looking for us.

Chief Krampf slid over to my position, "Boy! You really hit it out of the park this time, Rick. Real good intelligence on this one." His eyes were wild and you could easily tell he was excited.

"Yeah, I'm pretty damned impressed too. Although we still have a lot on our plate to deal with."

Eric wasn't even a little concerned. "And deal with them, we will, Rick. Man! This is great. What a blast. Thanks for the invite." He gave me a sharp slap on the back and moved off back towards the Team Commander. They were going to have to develop a plan for the night action now that it was pretty clear we couldn't be extracted tonight.

None of them were scared? Was I the only one? No, couldn't be. They had to be keeping their own fears and apprehensions to themselves. This is not so much bravado as it is a necessity. Fear can be a contagious virus that will infect a whole team and make them virtually useless. I've seen it happen before. Eric moved off and I was grateful for his brief but inspiring visit.

Ryan caught my eye and motioned me over to his position. I crawled over and slid in beside him. "Hey Rick, here's what we are going to do. We can't afford to let them bring their numbers down on us in a swell, so when they get within five or six hundred meters of us, we are going to open up with the 240's, this is a light machine-gun, crew served, 7.62mm that replaced the old M-60, it fires about 500 to 700 rounds per minute, and has a range of about a thousand meters, we had two of them, when they get within four hundred meters, we'll start out with the SAWs Squad Automatic Weapons=this is a 5.56mm very light machine gun, also crew served, almost identical to the M-240 except smaller, with a maximum effective range or almost 800 meters, fires about 600 to 800 rounds per minute, we had two of these also. Once they are within 300, we'll open up with our small arms. We have to keep them as far away as possible for as long as possible. Do you understand?" Basically he was saying what is a typical infantry procedure in the defense. That in about five minutes, we going to get personally engaged.

"Roger."

"Make sure you keep eye contact with our security team out there on your right. We may reel them in come nightfall."

"Roger."

"Good job today, Rick. You really earned your money here."

"Thanks Ryan. You're not one to sling around praise undeservedly, so that means a lot."

"Let's just hope we've taken the wind out of their sails here."

"Now don't go getting all teary-eyed and misty on me, Ryan. I wouldn't know how to handle it."

He patted me on the shoulder and I slithered out to my previous position.

We all watched as the heard seemed to grow with this long pause in the fire. I saw what Ryan was doing with this pause, because it was working perfectly. They were starting to cluster together again forming larger pockets. However, they were also now moving some tactical prowess. When they were about 800 meters from us, Ryan opened up with the artillery again, putting it just about at the rear of their cluster, and this made them start moving towards us with a little more speed and purpose. Those that were in the rear of the formations all dropped and tried to ride out the Artillery storm, while those in front tried to watch the whole scene over their shoulders while they were running straight for us. I have to admit, he had them packaged for destruction very nicely. True to his word, at 700 meters, he ordered the M-240's to open fire but be very conservative with ammunition.

The gunners opened up, firing nice controlled six to nine round bursts. Now with the artillery pounding them on the east side, us shooting at them from the west side, they were left with the only option of spread out and flatten out, or take us out. Now the cat was out of the bag, too. They now knew we were here, and where we were. The good thing, or maybe it wasn't, was that night fall would be soon upon us. Brother, do we own the night.

Their leadership could be seen moving amongst them, trying to get them up and moving towards us. Wherever one was identified, one was killed. It was just that systematic. To close with us, and take us out. This was the only way out. When their leadership presented themselves, they were rewarded with small packages of copper jacketed lead. A few of the small unit leaders tried numerous times to get their squads up and moving with limited success. Once they were within 500 meters, Ryan had the SAWs open up and rake over the bounding formations. Again, being conservative on ammo, because it was surely going to be a very long night.

"Rick, call back to the OPCEN and have them send out that kicker palette we put together," Ryan shouted to me. Prior to our leaving on this mission, we assembled a palette consisting of medical supplies, IVs, bandages, painkillers, radio batteries, and an ass load of ammunition for every weapon system we carried, mortar rounds, belted machine-gun ammo, rifle and pistol ammo, in addition to food and water, and everybody's treat: Claymores! Who doesn't want Claymores? Huh? Nobody here! We all want Claymores! Give us more Claymores! We all want Claymores!

In the event of an emergency, we would call for this palette to be flown out to us by chopper and kicked out hence the name kicker palette over our position. The only problem with that is, that sometimes, depending on the terrain, it can be a real ass pain trying to carry all of that stuff back to your position or hide, under fire!

I got back on the SATCOM radio, "Bastard, one-one, this is November, niner-niner, over?" Whatever code name the deployment is tasked with, determines starting letter of all the code names, hence the code name, Binkey. 'B' is a good letter for this. 'Z' is without a doubt, the worse! Actually, the OPCEN's code name was BASTRD and they filled in another vowel. Operators have a great deal of fun creating their own variations, i.e. BITCHS, BLOWME, etc. As long as it has no repeating characters...but yeah, they picked that one deliberately the same reason I picked Binkey.

"November niner-niner, this is Bastard, go ahead."

"It looks like we are going to be here a bit longer than expected. We are going to need that kicker palette sent out, ASAP. We're going to start loosing light in a couple of hours."

"Roger, November niner-niner. Do you have a BDA Battle Damage Assessment=this is a count of our sensitive items such as crypto, radios, night vision goggles, weapons and personnel for us?"

I looked over all of the dead bodies that littered the square, the steps to the mosque, the mud huts, the qalats; it was all very... ghastly! A pale blue haze hung in the air, but was thinning rapidly with the breeze. I could feel the cordite biting into my nostrils and eyes. I could feel the metallic taste at the back of my throat that comes from a massive expenditure of ammunition. Everybody's faces had the black traces of cordite, collected at the corners of the eyes, the around the lips and black streaks running down their faces where sweat dragged it down to their necks and chins. I covered everybody's hands and uniforms. Such are the post battle sights.

"Roger, at this time we have no casualties, we are green good on all sensitive items and equipment and about 150 rounds per man. We have between two and three hundred Enemy KIA, so far"

I heard cheering going on in the background when the jubilant voice came back on, "We'll be happy to get that palette out to you guys as soon as possible. We have another squadron of Apaches warming up to come your way as well. We'll put the palette on that sortie."

"Roger."

* * * *

19:00

Light was failing fast, and we saw them shouting back and forth to each other, while lying down, trying to find a break in the fire to move on us. Every so often, a squad size element would all stand at once and make a mad dash to move forward. And they would make it too. Close the distance between us by just a little more. However, they were still almost 500 meters from us. Our machine guns, continued to work them over sparingly.

The artillery had to shift their fires over in support of another unit under fire, so we gave them up, grudgingly. In the mean time we were using some mortars from the 82nd Airborne Division to keep them from fleeing back into Pakistan. We kept that wall of white hot steel razor blades a reality to their east, and we pounded them pretty good with smoke to their front. The problem with smoke is, while they can't see us, we can't see them either. They were close enough to us now, that if we were to call in a fire mission to our front, to engage their closest elements, we would be at 'Danger Close'. This is a term that indirect fire units use to warn those of us requesting Danger Close missions that we are in danger of hitting our own folks.

"Rick! Bring that radio up here," Ryan called to me. I hated to crawl in and out of my position all of the time, not just because of the ass pain, but because it took another rifle, mine, off of the line.

I wormed and dragged my ruck up to him. The smoke is fine, but I'm going to put some more steel on them to try and keep them at distance for as long as possible."

"Sounds reasonable to me." He was already speaking to the mortar crews.

"This is November niner-one, got another mission for you. We're going to cancel the smoke. A linear target, spread it out over a 500 meter front, starting at the mountain pass at Pre-plot target number nine, running north east across my front. Danger Close."

"Bastard one-one, this is November niner-niner, do you have an ETA on that kicker, over?"

"The Apaches are still loading up with fresh ordinance. We'll give you a call when they are airborne."

I looked at Ryan, who looked incredibly sad, as though this whole thing might fall to pieces before his very eyes. It had been over an hour since I first called the OPCEN, and now we are told that 'the check is in the mail'. How typical.

Then that wall of steel came down from the 82nd Airborne Division's mortars, and that seemed to give him some reassurance. It certainly took some of the fight out of the Taliban, because they fell back about fifty meters and tried to regroup, while about twenty-five percent of them on the Taliban left front, our right, seemed to think that now was a good time to make a break for the pass and the J-Bad road. Several dozen all seemed to hesitate for a second, and then made their dash. Our security team opened up on them with automatic fire. Not the mad uncontrolled rattle of wasted ammunition, but the controlled, well-aimed bursts. Before anybody got within a hundred meters of the pass, they were either dead, or rethinking that decision on the run.

Because of that escape attempt, Ryan yelled to the FDC Fire Direction Center, "That linear target, shift to the right and fire all guns! Danger close!"

The ground just shook with the new fire mission.

In the meantime, the Taliban was getting very tired of being pounded. Somebody blew a whistle and they all seemed to stand in mass and begin charging forward. Spraying wildly with their AKs. No longer were they moving in bounds or rushes. When they stood, we saw just how many of them were left with fighting spirit. It was way too many. I'm just guessing at maybe eight or nine hundred. This was something out of WWII Japanese Banzai charges. They were just now approaching 400 meters out, which is a very long distance to charge. They were running, albeit not fast, but they couldn't have very much water left, if any. We had been pounding them for over six hours!

The crew served weapons went into overdrive. The Heavy Weapons man and his assistant started lobbing 60mm Mortar rounds on to the enemy's front elements using a direct lay technique. A wall of crazed humanity was streaming towards our tiny little position. Every few seconds a 60mm mortar round would strike in their ranks leaving a black and gray geyser of smoke and steel. When that smoke cleared there was a large gap in their ranks. *Hoo Yaahh!*

* * * *

19:10

At 400 meters, we all opened up. There front rank was very nearly decimated in a few seconds. In their world, they were really still not in effective range of us. With the optics that each man had on his weapon, 400 meters from a stable prone, stationary position, was little challenge. However, we were all aware of their numbers so we all used our ammo conservatively. Especially now that we had no idea when our palette would get there, if at all!

* * * *

19:20

Three hundred meters out and closing. *Nice, steady, well aimed shots, smile big... Good night! Nice one! On to the next one.* Some were trying desperately to take cover behind the numerous rock outcroppings but mostly behind the bodies of their fallen comrades. Some were trying to take a break from the battle while others were telling themselves they would never leave the safety of these rocks. Now that their advance had slowed to a crawl, our mortar man began to target each outcroppingone at a time, with amazing results—he took away their safe-havens.

It wasn't long before my eyes could feel the sting of the cordite, with every swallow I tasted the acrid bitter taste of the spent gunpowder. I could feel it getting gritty on my teeth. I saw the haze from the spent ammunition and through it, I saw the orange muzzle flashes of the wall of AKs as they advanced on us. Rounds continued to chip away at the stone in front of us, the whining "pang" as they bounced off of the stone behind us, seemed to reverberate through the air.

A small cluster of Taliban rose up out of a small depression in the ground that we hadn't seen before now, and they made a desperate break to rush us. But they were still too far out, and were cut down within seconds. They must've crawled their way into that depression under the cover of the smoke and stayed there waiting for a lull in our fire. *Sucks to be them.*

* * * *

19:34
Two hundred meters, and closing much quicker than I would have like. They are close enough now that we can see their beards, their anger, their fear, their everlasting final moments. No longer was our fire sporadic. We were firing at a steady constant rate and their ranks thinned only for a second. The SAW gunners poured it on like never before. The machine-gunners were on the verge of running out of ammo. They had carried twice a basic load this time, because we thought that it could be a prolonged fight, plus we weren't planning on having to move very far. Now, they were linking together their last few belts.

Constantly, the loud reverberating "Crack" of a bullet as it passes overhead, could be heard with a nearly equal number of loud *pang* sounds as the bullets ricocheted off of the rocks behind us. Nobody got away without having chipped rock fragments to the face as bullets glanced off of our front cover.

Apparently the Taliban had decided to use their remaining RPGs against us, rather than save them for our air assets. Several of them started streaking across the night sky, impacting and exploding on the rocks behind us. Everybody was showered with fragments and rock. We had eaten at least fifteen RPG rockets when they ran out.

"Shit! I'm hit. Dave? Dave?" Since I was on the far right, it came from my left.

I heard Clark answer back, "Yeah, where did you get it?"

"My neck and back."

"Hold tight, I'll be right there."

"November niner-niner, this is Tomahawk, two-two, over?" The SATCOM sprang to life unexpectedly.

"Tomahawk, two-two, I wasn't expecting you, where are you from?" This was encrypted communications so we could almost talk as though we were on the phone. Only the Army seems to have the over and out hang ups.

"USS Nimitz, just returning from a TIC Troops in contact with the Marines down near Chamkani, I have a little ordinance left, mostly 20mm cannon and a couple of rockets. I may as well burn it up before I refuel at Bagram."

"Roger, Stand by." I yelled for Ryan, then I crawled over to his position dragging my rucksack and radio, "Got a fast mover from the Nimitz, Tomahawk twenty-two, who wants to visit," and I handed him the handset, and crawled back to my nitch.

"Tomahawk twenty-two, this is November ninety-one, my position is 42 Sierra X-ray Delta 3915 7989, I got 'em in real close, if you could give me a couple of gun runs going from southwest to northeast, I'd really appreciate it. We have the road through the mountain pass closed off, but I think that's where they are trying to break through."

"How close are they November ninety-one?"

"This guy in the hole here with me tried to pick my pocket a minute ago."

"Roger, November ninegy-one, I'm still about twomikes out." Two mikes, meaning two minutes.

"Awww, Christ! I'm hit! The voice came from my left, again. It sounded like Dave Clark, a medic on the team.

"How bad is it?" Ryan asked.

"My arm."

"I'm on it, Ryan." That voice was Eric's.

Even in the almost diminished light, we could only see about two hundred meters down slope, but we could clearly see rank upon rank moving towards us with determination. But, within seconds of him saying it, the Taliban ranks suddenly started laying down as though somebody had taken a scythe through them, a half second later we heard the jet's machine-guns ripping them a new one. Then we heard the beast pass over head. We still had hundreds of them directly in front of us, since he seemed to focus his gun run on the rear ranks, presumably not wanting to get too close to us. I can appreciate that.

"Rick! Come get this radio! I can't talk to these guys right now," Ryan seemed to be in a better mood, despite the circumstances. He wasn't feeling quite so desperate anymore.

The F-18 came in for another run, this time, to keep the Pakistani passes closed. Here, he expended all of his remaining rockets. My oldest son, Jason had served on the Nimitz for eight years when he was in the Navy. *God Bless the Nimitz*, I thought to myself as I wormed my way out of my cover and crawled over to Ryan, then took the ruck and the handset. As soon as he handed it to me, I heard the OPCEN calling.

"November niner-niner, this is Bastard one-one, we just got word Tango, two eight is airborne and en-route to your location with a bunch of goodies. How copy, over?"

"Roger, Bastard. Goodies en-route to our pos."

"Ryan, the Apaches are coming back and they must have a slick non-gunship with our kicker palette."

"Well, it's about time."

The F-18 came around for his last gun run, his rounds kicked up so much dust and grit and he was bringing in to within a hundred meters of us. I could feel all the dust and fine bits of rock caking up on my teeth. On the other hand, it could have been that way all afternoon, but I just now noticed it.

"November ninety-nine, this is Tomahawk twenty-two, that's it for me. I'm bone dry. I hope I helped."

"Brother, you have no idea! You were just what the doctor ordered. Have a nice one!"

"November ninety-nine, this is Tango twenty-eight, we are now about five mikes out from your position. I hear it's pretty hairy down there. What's your status, over?"

"Well, the guy I'm talking to has green eyes. Do you want to talk him?"

"No, I'll take your word for it."

"We are loosing light fast. Ammunition is at a critical state. I wonder where it all went to."

"Roger, hang on for a few more minutes."

The Taliban fire was now less than half of what it was a few minutes ago. I looked over the whole battlefield and saw bodies all over the terrain, from Pakistan all the way up to where we were laying, where they laid in layers upon layers. How many were still left was a good question, because I suspect there were a lot of them out there, playing opossum.

After the F-18 broke off, and there was nothing else in the sky, some of those opossums must've felt emboldened, because several of them stood up and once again, started moving forward. Their firepower picked up again, just when you thought there could be many more, several hundred made themselves and their displeasure of us, known.

I heard the thumping of chopper blades in the distance and so could the Taliban.

"Bastard eleven, this is November ninety-nine. Lift all fires; I say again. Lift all fires. We have birds inbound."

"Roger, November ninety-nie. Lifting all supporting fires."

So it went. It was as though somebody had flipped a switch. Suddenly, there was no more sound of incoming mortars or artillery. Only sound of approaching rotor blades. In this pause, this brief unscripted and unplanned cease fire, even the Taliban seemed to stop and pause, to look over the mountain side where our position was, to look beyond the top. The air was electric. There was a charge in the air that something ominous was going to occur.

Then, at the end of this brief four or five second pause, something did. The flight of seven Apache helicopters flew into view of all of us on the battlefield, and almost immediately, all them seemed to be firing rockets, upon rockets upon rockets. In this same instant, their 30mm chain operated machine-guns gave long and loud burps, as they spit the long orange ropes of tracer fire into the now fleeing Taliban. The smoke trails from the rockets glowed against the pitch black of night. The rockets plowed huge rows and gapes through the Taliban ranks. A couple of times I saw an RPG shoot up into the sky in a wild desperate reach to hit a chopper, but they all flew wide this night. The pilots must've been flying with NVGs because, even though they were firing over our heads, nothing ever landed on us. For which we were immensely grateful.

On the heels of the Apaches came a twin rotor CH-47 with our kicker palette. He came over us slow and then hovered for a moment and began a decent. He got about as low to the ground as he could with out clipping the mountain side as it rose up behind us. I could clearly see the crewmen in the red light of the cabin shove the palette out about fifteen feet above the ground. With water and ammunition, it was several hundred pounds. It crashed to the ground and the cardboard sides split open despite the steel banding. The crewmen gave us all a wave and thumbs up as we watched the huge chopper rise up, pivot about and lift up over the mountain, out of sight.

Now that the Taliban were on the run, several of us went up and began carrying supplies back to our position.

* * * *

19:48
One hundred meters and closing. Ryan yelled out, "Keep your heads down, we have an F-18 coming in for a gun run!"

Why did they have to be so damned close? This noise! This cacophony! The roar of their AKs, the steady rip and crash of our weapons, the periodic thunder of our 40mm Grenade rounds, the exhaustion, the hunger, the steady unquenchable thirst, all of it, kept us from concentrating. All of it a distraction when you could afford none. Decisions came tough. *Oh, I could use a cup of coffee and a few minutes of quiet.*

However, none was to be had; the enemy was only fifty meters away at this point and nobody had time to think. It was all; *sights, aim, relax, slow trigger squeeze...next target...reload.* We heard the Taliban shouting back and forth amongst themselves and see their mouths moving as they spat what I imagined to be a steady stream of profanity against us. That's fine with me, stick and stones...

I heard both Ryan's and Eric's voices above the din, "Fix Bayonets!" By this time, the enemy couldn't have been more than twenty-five meters away, perhaps fifteen in some places. Up and down the line, the steady clicking and clacking could be faintly heard over the din of the battle, as men clicked and locked their bayonets into place. I did the same thing. I also heard Ryan on the radio calling for flares. We'd need every advantage we could get to have a bayonet fight at night against a vastly numerically superior force.

I watched as a cluster of seven or eight were closing on me less than twenty meters away, I still had a couple of grenades left so I decided to give them one, letting the safety lever, or 'spoon' fly, I counted out, *one thousand, two thousand three thousand,* of their standard five second fuse. In that three second count they had closed to within ten meters, I hurled the grenade at the closest and struck him squarely in the chest. I watched him clutch his chest with both hands and stagger backwards, as I sank toward the bottom of my hole, I heard the blast, felt the concussive force, the shower of dirt grit and bone as I rose back up to look back and found they were replaced by numerous heaps of rags. *Battlefield littering. It's a tragic thing.* For a second, I remembered going through bayonet training as an Infantryman at North Harmony Church at Fort Benning, back in 1979. Our Instructor screamed the question, "Men! What is the spirit of the Bayonet?"

In response, we all cried, "To Kill! To Kill! To Kill Without Mercy!" A dozen times he had us yell this chant. *So it is said, so it is done.*

As the first artillery flares burst and burned over our positions, I saw several trying to push themselves back up and several behind them move up to fill the void in their ranks, I sprang from my hole with the stock of my M-4 pressed to my hip, weapon at a forty-five degree angle, leading with my bayonet, trail foot diagonal to the attack, left arm locked. I lunged at one who tried to fill hole I'd made.

Parry! Thrust! Withdraw! Square in the chest. Resisitance. Relax. Dump the body! Move on! On Guard! I have to be much faster. Block! Butt stroke! Parry. Thrust. Withdraw. On Guard. Block. Parry. Thrust. Withdraw. Parry, guard...block-parry-thrust-withdraw-onguard. Parry through. Withdraw. On guard!

I glimpse the sight of Eric springing from his hole with an entrenching tool in one hand and a 9mm Beretta in the other, and he swung that entrenching tool down with savage force, striking a shit head, in the head with the edge so hard, in my mind's eye, I saw the two halves sink toward his shoulders. In reality, he dropped like a stone. Eric wasted no time in moving on to the next lucky winner. He moved with a speed and agility that I would not have believed of such a large man. *Back to my own troubles...*

Time seemed to stop and became a blur of unending bodies coming forth for the slaughter. It was all a mass of tangled limbs, hands pulling at my arms, legs and uniform, rifle muzzles jammed at ribs and torso, stocks clashed with my arms, blurred grimy faces, eyes wide in hatred and anger. *Fine. Right back atchya fuck-face! Butt Stroke! Butt Stroke! Butt Stroke! BlockPeryThrustWithdraw, Block. Parry. Thrust. Withdraw... Butt stroke. Butt Stroke. Butt Stroke. Block. Parry. Thrust. Withdraw. Block. Parry. Thrust. Withdaw.* The entire planet

Earth, my whole existence, had been reduced to the one square yard of earth that I was standing on. *Block. Parry. Thrust. Withdraw. Block, parry, thrust, withdraw...* It seemed to go on like this for *hours...*

Eventually, the number of men moving against me seemed to thin. As soon as I had a second and a half, I reloaded and killed the two closest to me then took aim on the next one, after him, the rest seemed to melt away. I looked over to my right to see Kevin just five meters away, bloody and smiling and alive. I looked to my left to see Eric and Ryan had advanced into the melee and were now a good seventy meters in front of our positions. Gradually as the slaughter lost steam, I saw that everybody had left their positions. I looked back to my position to see that we all had advanced on the shitheads at least fifty meters.

As though some distant whistle had blown, we all stopped, paused then walked back to our positions. I heard Ryan ask Eric, "Do you need more pistol ammo?" referring to the 9mm in Eric's hand.

I saw Eric shake his head, "Nahhh, I never fired it. I just used this," and he held up the small folding shovel.

Ryan chuckled, "Why did you bring it with you?"

As though it were the stupidest question he'd ever heard, "I'm signed for it."

* * * *

20:30

The Apaches stayed on station and continued to work the Taliban over where ever they found them.

"Rick, I need you to come up here for a minute," Ryan spoke out loud. Once again, I slithered my way over.

"Sir."

"We got some dead space down there about three hundred meters to our one o'clock." He was referring to the depression which had concealed several men earlier. Dead space is an Infantryman's term which means ground which cannot be covered with direct fire weapons such as machine-guns and rifles. Ravines, creeks or holes are considered dead space requiring something to drop down on to them.

"What do you have in mind?"

"I'm thinking that I want you to go over by the security team, move down the mountain and cross over the J-Bad road, then take a position on that far side that will afford you a view into that depression. You'll still be outside of our sectors of fire and you'll be along side the security team so there's no problem coming from them."

"Okay, whose going with me?"

"I'm thinking of sending you with Kevin. He'll watch your back while you watch that depression. I'll take your SATCOM from you and give you one of the walkie-talkies. Sound good to you?"

"Sounds fine. I'll yank the SATCOM out."

Kevin Stubben came up a moment later and Ryan went through his plan again. When he had us both there, he went on further.

"The shit heads already know we are here. What I might do is, shift the team over to that side of the pass in ones and twos before daylight. I'll let you know when we put that into effect."

With that, Kevin and I moved out. I didn't know Kevin very well. I knew he'd been in the Army for ten years and was a Sergeant First Class. I knew he was a medic and by all accounts a damned good one. I knew he came from Youngstown, Ohio. He had a tendency to rub some people wrong. But then again, so did I. *Yeah, imagine that...* A little abrasive, they would say. From what I did know, he was one of the best soldiers I'd ever known. I've known a few in nearly thirty years. With-out saying a word, we moved up to the security element, told them what we were doing, then began our descent.

* * * *

22:00

While we had only moved a kick or so, it was over some very rugged terrain, and we moved with maximum stealth. At no time, did we see anybody else. Not on the road and not when we got to the other side. The moon was out now and the stars shine bright. It was much easier to move now, but we still took our time. There was a large thick belt of stars that ran through the sky that made people say it was the prettiest they'd ever seen. I've seen better though—in the Middle-East in 1984.

Kevin and I stayed in the rocks and skirted around the pass back toward the contact side of the mountain, but now south of the J-Bad road. Once we had the field of vision that we needed, we began a gradual ascent up the mountainside to gain elevation and improve our field of fire.

22:30

Kevin and I found a position that was satisfactory to the both of us, and had enough of level shelf to hold the rest of the team, if and when Ryan decided to bring them over. After we were relatively comfortable, Kevin and I began whispering our tall tales. It only took about five minutes for me to like this guy and to understand that he was completely misunderstood. Granted, like me, he was abrasive. His sense of humor was almost identical to mine on several different levels. We spent most of the next hour breathless in silent, painful, stifled, gut retching laughter.

When Kevin who had also been raised Catholic, explained how he got expelled from Catholic Kindergarten for throwing a pair of scissors at a nun, it was too much to bear. I suddenly had visions of a much smaller Kevin being dragged by the ear, across the classroom, down the hall, and tossed into the Mother Superior's Office, again by the ear, to face the flying ruler O' fury!

* * * *

22:48
Our two man comedy when through the NVGs I observed thirty-five to forty Taliban crawling on all fours along the base of the mountain. Approximately fifteen of them crawled up hill into the slight depression that we had observed earlier in the day.

I raised Ryan on the small Motorola, "Ryan, this Rick, you've got about forty of them crawling around in front of you. They are now about 250 meters down slope from you."

"Roger, Rick. Let me know what their up to, or when they decide to make a push. Do you have that dead space covered?"

"Roger."

"Keep me posted."

* * * *

23:10
A second group of shit heads came up behind the first group, about the same in number, and they just seemed to settle in the rocks at the base of the mountain. I informed Ryan that he now had between seventy and eighty men to his front. One rank at 250 meters and another at 300 meters.

* * * *

23:25
A third group, much smaller in number, crawled along the base of the mountain but continued on passed the depression, which was about their extreme left flank. But this group of twenty or so, crawled for nearly another hundred meters. They looked as if they were poised to make a break for the pass. I called the security team and Ryan, and gave them both a heads up.

* * * *

23:40
Several of the first rank began to rise to their feet, tentatively at first, but eventually they all stood at a crouch, and began a slow walk up hill towards Ryan's position. The second rank slowly rose, and moved forward, to roughly the positions of the previous group. I called Ryan and told him to expect company, and that it looked like they were going to try to assault in two waves.

I watched as they made their slow somewhat stealthy climb of the mountainside, and I watched as they got within a hundred meters of Ryan's position, and I couldn't figure out why Ryan didn't open up on them. They all had to be able to see them through the NVGs, as plain as day! At this point, the second rank also stood and began a stealthy climb up hill towards Ryan.

When the first rank was within fifty meters of them, I began to sight in on one of them thinking that for some reason, Ryan had gone insane and that I was going to have to start this engagement. When all at once, a series of explosions rocked the far mountainside, pierced by pitched, howling, blood curling screams nearly a dozen brilliant flashes of light from the fusillade of hand grenades they had been thrown, simultaneous to this, the second rank broke into a slow run up hill, over the uneven rocky slope, and the third cluster that had poised nearest the entrance to the pass, stood up and broke into a slow trot, there were a few determined men of the first rank who still lurched forward and screamed their fury, *"Allah Aq Baaarrrh!"*

There were several responding bursts of automatic fire. "Ryan, they're on the move, everybody's moving. Security team, that group is coming your way!"

Ryan was as calm as could be. "Let 'em come. We got somethin' for 'em."

Within seconds the second rank was within the fifty meter Ricker and they all let out their screams, and began their wild spraying of AK fire, when everybody, and I do mean everybody, cut loose with their Claymore mines, again bigger, brighter flashes of light peppered the mountainside, then there were a few shots, and then there were none.

Ryan must've called for some Illumination from the mortar crew because brilliant flares burst in the sky casting the eerie images of battle that last a lifetime. All the bodies in front of the team's position were piled a top each other, in all of their grotesque glory.

As the small group of twenty made their dash for the pass, the Security Team, must've just began tossing grenades wildly because four or five of them exploded in and around the small cluster. Then there was one well aimed shot. Then there was none.

From my vantage point, with light cast by the flares, it gave a very surreal feeling, as though you were observing something, moving through something, but not a part of it. The thin blue haze of gun smoke had returned and hung in the air about five feet off of the ground. Usually, this distinct, oil and water type separation occurs when moisture is rising up from the ground. Here, it was moisture rising up from the dead. However, as near as I could tell, there was not a single survivor from that push. They would not soon try this again. And try again, they did not. Not for the rest of the night. For the rest of the night, Kevin and I traded off sleep and watching in one hour shifts.

* * * *

Thursday, 20 August 2009
04:00

When the night was at its darkest, Ryan decided to shift the team over to our location. He did this in teams of two. To include the Security Team, they also moved over to the south side of the J-Bad road. Everybody immediately began to string out new Claymores to the front of their positions.

I found that we now had a third wounded man from that last push. Steven took a round to the chest but was stable and coherent. Doc Clark helped carry him across and monitored him throughout.

* * * *

04:50

Yet, another cluster of Taliban was observed crawling along the base of the mountainside and then began moving up to a point about 200 meters from where the team's previous position was located. This was a fairly large group of about fifty men.

They were in for a little disappointment.

* * * *

05:15
Light was up enough to where we could see with relatively little effort. Just a little residual gray remained of the night. The NVGs were no longer necessary, and we watched as the Taliban stood and began another assault on our old position. Ryan was talking to the artillery, "Okay, are you standing by with that Battery 6 mission?"

"That's a roger. We'll fire on your command."

"Fire. Fire all guns, now!"

Within seconds, the swilling growl of the 155 rounds pouring through the air could be heard, just about as the Taliban was nearly twenty-five meters from our old position, the rounds started impacting. The gray geysers with the brilliant white shower of sparks showed that Ryan's taste was for Willy Peter today. A few made to our empty location and turned back around and ran down hill, not wanting to play anymore. About thirty remained and were now running down hill away from the old position as fast as possible over the rocks. Ryan shifted fire.

"Shift right five zero, and let 'em have it again."

The second barrage landed, slightly in front of Ryan's correction. He compensated for their fast footwork, "Shift right five zero again, and pour it on."

He kept up the artillery until the last eight survivors ducked into a mud hut compound, at which point he changed the fire mission to HE and let go for another twenty minutes. We really had no idea how many were left on the battlefield before us. We got glimpses of single individuals running from cover to cover, periodically throughout the morning. We were now more or less waiting for their next move.

* * * *

11:15
"November ninety-nine, this is Bastard eleven. What's your

current status, over?"

"Right now, we are occupying new positions on the south of the J-Bad road, we still have all of our sensitive items, crypto and weapons. At this time, we have three wounded, one serious, and the others ambulatory and we are still good on ammunition."

"Roger, we have a predator unmanned arial vehicle—UAV going to your location and it came up with some very interesting developments. It would appear that you have a rather large relief column on its way to you, to help liberate their friends."

"How large of a force are we talking about?"

"We estimate it to be roughly a Battalion size column of cars, trucks and even a couple of buses. I think we are talking about three hundred to four hundred men coming your way."

I moved over to Ryan and told him, "Bastard thinks we have about four hundred shit heads coming our way. They're tracking them on predator."

"Bastard this is November ninety-one, how far out are they?"

"Tough to say, perhaps twenty or thirty minutes."

"Will you be able to provide with some additional assistance?"

"We'll see what we can do." They signed off. This was not good news.

I'd been scared plenty during the night. I'd been scared that I would be wounded, suffer an amputation, suffer another head wound, which in my case would be terminal and at some moments, that I might actually be killed. Now, for the first time, I thought about my wife, Kathie, about our kids, and my two way too precious grandchildren, and the third that was due in October. *Nope, this is no time to think of them. You have to stay focused. You're not getting planted here!*

* * * *

11:35

I was right. "November ninety-one, this is Bastard, over?"

"Go ahead Bastard, this is ninety-one," Ryan replied.

"Our gift to you should be arriving at your position at any minute. We decided to give you the gift of the overwhelming air power of the United States Air Force. You'll see what I mean when it gets there."

Colonel Jones was such a clown sometimes. True to his word, a Blackhawk chopper called us on the radio, not three minutes later asking for a fix on our location, saying they were two mikes out.

* * * *

11:38
Staff Sergeant Gus Samuels, Mississippi Air National Guard, fast rope rappelled down to our position from the hovering Blackhawk overhead. He had his radio on his back already and his equipment was tossed down a second later. Samuels was one of the Air Force TAC-Ps. These are Tactical Combat Air Controllers, and usually this means that we have the ear of a Spooky Gunship. After throwing his gear out, the Blackhawk lifted to its left and took off over the mountain.

A Spooky gunship is much like the old Specter gunships or the older ones seen in movies, like *Puff the Magic Dragon* in *The Green Berets*, these AC-130 Gunships carry more firepower than they ever dreamed of in Hollywood. To include cannon! Gus had his radio up in minutes. Several of us went to the edge of the pass to get a glimpse of what was coming our way from the west. Needless to say, we were not amused.

"I hate to say this guys, but under the ROE Rules of Engagement, we have to receive a hostile act from that column before we can engage them." This too, was not what we wanted to hear.

We could see several miles although the terrain wasn't flat, we saw a column of vehicles coming our way with a trail of dust so high and so thick, they probably couldn't go faster than thirty miles an hour so as not to hit each other.

Ryan said, "That's easy." He spoke into the Motorola walkie-talkie, "Security Team, once that column from the west get's within ranger, fire a few warning shots over their head and let's see what they do."

"Roger," came the reply.

When they were between 300-400 meters out, they fired a few shots in front of the lead Hilux pick up. When that didn't seem to impress them, they fired three shots over the heads of the passengers in the back, and this didn't impress them so much that they fired half a belt of ammunition from an RPK machine-gun that was on the roof of the cab."

"How's that for a hostile act?" Ryan asked Gus.

"I like that just fine. Then he spoke into his radio "Sierra seven-seven, are you on station?"

"Affirmative. We just arrived. We are looking at that column now. It would seem you've made some people pretty angry."

"Brother, you don't know the half of it. You should see what it looks like from here. But they just fired on us, so you are clear to engage at anytime."

Now with the lead vehicle less than a quarter mile from the pass, Spooky began to mop the length of the J-Bad road with a long rope of red tracer fire. It was like nothing I've ever seen before. Vehicle flipped and turned off of the road, piled into each other, bodies fell out of trucks, ran across the desert floor, only to be sucked down into it by a cloud of 40mm cannon impacting rounds at a rate of nearly 4,000 rounds per minute. In less than three minutes, nearly all of those three hundred were dead.

Ryan called us all back over to our positions and we now turned our attention back to our front, where apparently the Taliban wanted to make one more try for the pass. They would've been much better off running to Pakistan. We watched as they emptied out of three separate compounds and formed up behind the adobe walls of the last compound they had for cover.

Their right flank came out first, followed by the middle and then the left. Unbelievably, there were still nearly a hundred of them left. They were making large bounds of at least a hundred meters with each bound, although they weren't firing, yet. They were still trying to close the distance.

Gus said into his radio, "Hey Sierra, can you bring it around to the east side of the mountain and take a look at what we're seeing."

"Roger...I see what you have there. Do we have confirmation that these are bad guys?"

"That's a roger. They've been slugging it out with the team here all night."

"'Ats good enough for me. Stand by, we're going to swing around and come at this from the north, so we don't hit that mosque."

There was a point where two of the three groups were prone, laying on their fronts 'covering' the middle group as it advanced. This was when Spooky came along and stitched them to the carpet with another string of 40mm cannon rounds. The Middle group then seemed to disperse, no longer interested in us, and only in saving their skins. Can't blame 'em. Spooky came around again and took them all out in groups of three, then groups of two and then finally one by one. We made called the OPCEN and gave them the phase line code to bring in the conventional force for mop up. This was a battalion from the 82nd Airborne Division that would search for and treat survivors, and prisoners, and gather all weapons. As their CH-47 loomed on the horizon we packed our gear to climb on one, just as soon as they climbed off.

* * * *

16:00
Back at Jalallabad Airfield JAF, I knew the Brigadier would want a report by morning but this report was going to be too tiring to write. I was sitting at the aid station with several others from the team while our friends were treated. They'd all be going to Germany and then to the states. I stepped outside and a little girl of perhaps seven years old was eyeing me from about ten feet away. I was suddenly conscious of my appearance. My uniform was almost didn't resemble a uniform at all; I was soaked through to the skin with sweat and blood. Mostly sweat, it was shredded and completely brown with dust and grit, except for the front which was doused in blood, my hands were caked with it fortunately none of it mine, dirt and sand was caked all over my skin where it mixed with dried sweat. I sat on a bench outside the aid station and pulled an MRE Chocolate bar from the cargo pocket of my trousers; I unwrapped it and offered it to her. Her mother was a few feet away trying to explain to a medic what was wrong with her son of about three or four.

The little girl walked up to me and began speaking to me in Pashto then she smiled big, took the candy bar, took a bite, and made the Hhhmmm sound that we all make, then she pulled up a seat right next to me on the bench and I opened my canteen and let her have my water. It was as if this was the only natural place to be—next to the ugly bloody beast.

* * * *

Friday, 21 August 2009
09:00
Back at Bagram Airfield, sitting in the J-2 section's coffee room, still completely wiped out from the weeks labor. I was aware of Moneypenny's presence at the counter and I listened as she fixed herself a 'brew' cup of tea in British speak. As she turned to leave I felt her hand on my shoulder. "I'm very glad to see you again, Master Sergeant," she said. I was going to ignore her, but now I couldn't resist the temptation any longer.

I looked up at her, "Thank you, Moneypenny. So, how are you?"

With a totally impassive face, completely devoid of any emotion or humor, she said, "When I'm on top? Quite excellent! An animal, even."

"I bet you are," I replied.

Then she gave me a wave of her fingers again and said, "Toodles."

She smiled so brightly, and I merely looked back down into my coffee and let her go. I could tell by the cadence of her steps that she was swaying her hips, boldly as she sometimes did. Since there was nobody else in the room, I knew she was doing it for my benefit, but I wasn't going to give her the satisfaction of catching me looking.

Chapter Six

Week ending 8/29/09
Monday, 23 August 2009. 01:50

The three loud *kahrump* sounds roused most of us at FOB Forward Operating Base Mehtar Lam. Most of us in the Special Forces compound the purpose of this tiny little SF outpost in the middle of a larger FOB was just to support other SF missions, which is what I was still technically assigned to, came to our courtyard and divided the workload. The three Chinese made 107mm Rockets had detonated, one on the chopper pad, one near the mess hall, and one outside the wire, the outer edge of the FOB.

There was no pandemonium. Not even really any excitement, so common an occurrence was it, I grabbed the most Junior Enlisted Soldier on our compound, Specialist Derek Easely. "Okay, Derek. You stay here, man that firing position up on top."

Derek nodded and moved toward the position.

For Ron, our OIC Officer in Charge a Signal Corps Officer this means he was a computer and communications nerd, by no means a combat officer, or even a real leader, "Ron, you stay here and man the OPCEN. Krash referring to Mike Simons, nick name, a motor sergeant you spell Derek every twenty or thirty minutes. I don't think anything else is coming this way, but be on your toes for the next few hours. Kevin *yes, the same Kevin Stubben of Youngstown, Ohio* and I are going to put together a patrol and try to find these bastards before they bug out."

Kevin had already grabbed his aid bag and thrown it in one of our Ford Rangers. We collected three of our terps and then drove to the OPCEN for the FOB which is not to be confused with our OPCEN which is located in our little tiny corner of the FOB. If these guys were smart, they'd already be gone. Sometimes, they're pretty stupid.

We stepped into the FOB's OPCEN and saw the entire night shift huddled around one TV screen as they scanned the surrounding landscape for our Rocketeers. This is what the "Big Army" meaning conventional forces does for security. "We'll just put CCTV cameras up there, so we can watch it from inside the

OPCEN." Actually, we normally have patrols our running around the FOB all night. But they timed this one just right between one patrols return and before the departure of the next. Not bad timing on their part.

"Are you guys going to send out a QRF Quick Reaction Force?" Kevin asked upon entry.

"No, we don't see anybody out there now," the Battle Captain replied. I looked at his name tag, Moore.

"Well, did you see anybody out there before the rockets hit?" I asked.

"Well, uhhh....no. But this camera only has a visibility for a thousand meters at night."

"Well, wouldn't that be the inherent problem with depending on a camera for your security?"

"Well, uhhh...I could see how you might think that."

Okay, this officer was going to try and make excuses for his shoddy outfit and I wanted no part of it. I'd already pointed out how stupid the idea was, now leave it alone.

"Well, we are going out into the Black Hills, to see if we can't find these guys. Do you have a few bodies for us? Anybody who wants to come with?" I knew there would be a cornucopia of volunteers. The chance to tell your kids that "I went on this one mission with Special Forces! It was top secret, but I'll tell you..." would be too much temptation for most of these FOBBITs *a pun on the Lord of the Rings saga; a FOBBIT is an armchair war hero who never leaves the safety and comfort of the FOB* pass up.

Three FOBBITs raised their hands right away. The Battle Captain picked who we could take, as four more raised their hands. The Captain allowed three to go with us.

"Do any of you have any combat experience?" This unit was a Cavalry unit from the Nevada National Guard and the only patches they had on their right sleeves was the same as the one of their left in the Army, it is custom to wear the patch of the unit you served in combat with on your right sleeve, and the unit you are currently assigned to on your left. They all shook their heads, 'No'.

Kevin, who used to be a Combat Engineer in the 82nd Airborne Division, 307th Engineers, before making his way to Special Forces he took the Medic's course only because it was the hardest, asked "What are your MOSs?" MOS refers to an individual's job in the Army, Military Occupational Specialty, i.e. Medic, Artillery, Armor, etc.

"Krash" and Derek were also ready to play. Having grown tired of being a rocket sponge, I collected my three Special Forces comrades and my three Nevada Guardsmen. Essentially, these are what we call "Legs," in the paratroops.

One answered, "I'm a commo guy." Commo being Army speak for communications.

The second said "I'm a nineteen kilo." This is the alpha-numeric code for a tracked vehicle crewman. Essentially of little use to us.

The third, stuck his chest out a little further and said rather boldly "Infantry". Unfortunately, as far out as he had stuck his chest, it still didn't stick out as far as his stomach.

Yes, he could be of value. "Okay, you three, follow us." We went outside and piled into our two Ford Rangers and headed for the 'Black Hills' which are the mountains to the north of the firebase. It was a natural choice for indirect fire because it could add a thousand meters, or so to your rocket. At the base of the hills, we dismounted the vehicles and scanned the hillsides with our NVGs. Nothing. We took a terp and talked to a few local nationals. They didn't hear anything. They were all awake though because it's Ramadan now, and they stay up all night eating, because they have to fast during the day.

We piled back in the trucks and headed east, the only remaining direction on the north side of the FOB from which they could fire. Again, we talked with a number of local nationals. Yes, they heard something. One heard a whoosh! Another heard it fly overhead. As we went to either side of these people, they didn't hear a thing. We were following the rockets' flight path. With no elevation in this direction, they had to be within a thousand meters of where we were now.

"Stallion Stable, this is Binkey; do you have a patrol outside the wire now?" I called back to the Cav's OPCEN.

"That's a negative, Binkey. We didn't want you guys to bump into each other." In fact, the Taliban frequently sets up ambushes on launch sites to trap the QRF or medical personnel sent to respond. So, I didn't have a problem with them not sending a QRF, but I had a great many issues in trying to replace eyes on the ground with CCTV. We drove to within about 700 meters of a large scrap yard that was now starting to look like a perfect launch site.

* * * *

03:00
Prior to leaving, I'd broken the patrol down into two elements. One Support and Security Element, One Assault Element. Kevin would take Krash and Derek and set up on the west side of their launch site, getting as close as they could. Once in position, I would take my Nevada Contingent along the southern edge of the shitheads. Then, all four of us would move forward until we made contact with the enemy. Krash and Derek would rake the launch site over with automatic fire from the Russian RPK Machine Gun Krash was carrying, and Derek would lob 40mm grenades down upon them using an M-203 we'd borrowed from the Nevada Guard. They would also ensure that *nobody*, absolutely *nobody*, entered or left the kill zone.

We all dismounted from the Fords, and took off on foot to close the distance quietly. It had been over an hour since they launched, and more than likely, they were gone. BUT! There was still a chance that since a QRF didn't come out, they may be feeling rather brazen.

Sure enough, Kevin on point, stopped the patrol. I came up to confer with him, to see what he saw. He raised his arm and pointed between rows of wrecked vehicles and broken bricks.

"I think I see movement over there," he said.

I peered through my goggles and, after a long minute, I heard a distinct metal on metal 'clank'.

"Well Kevin, there's somebody out there. Let's go say, 'Hi'."
He nodded silent agreement. He got his half of the patrol up and moved them out, to a supporting position. I gave him roughly fifteen minutes to get situated.

Then, I took my three and headed off toward the southern edge of the junk yard. I stopped every hundred meters to take a head count. Looking through my goggles, I could now see men readying rockets for a second launch. Once we were in line with them and approximately ninety degrees from where Kevin and Company should be set up. I halted the team and spread them out in a line

We were within a hundred meters of where they were. We heard a lot of metal on metal periodically and I clearly saw movement up ahead. We cleared the final row of junk and saw two men trying to handle another rocket out the back of a pickup, while one was rearranging clutter, trying to clear a field of fire or make a launching stand, whatever.

Kevin and I discussed it and we were pretty sure this wasn't a trap because I don't think they would've put their own people in the kill zone as bait. I put Kevin at one end of the line while I gradually pushed the other half forward. Kevin had one terp and I had one terp, and I had the dirty rotten nasty 'Legs!' *Paratroopers are funny this way and I make no apologies.* We were stretched out across fifty to seventy meters and creeping towards them with maximum stealth. I wanted to get within fifty meters, just so the chances of missing would be minimal.

While we were still over eighty meters away, I heard somebody stumble and a crash of metal on metal, then a loud, "Fuck!"

I looked down the rank and saw one of the Cav guys pushing himself up from his stomach. I was already pulling my trigger at the same time my eyes were just coming back around to the shitheads and the same instant Kevin had Krash and Derek open up loud and large.

My eyes immediately stayed focused on the four shitheads with the rocket, they were already piling into their truck. A burst from Krash's RPK disintegrated every piece of glass on the vehicle. One of Derek's grenades impacted just to the left of the launch site and slightly wounded one of them while I watched and reloaded.

Krash zeroed in on one of the rocketeers while he was tossing one into the bed of the truck. Krash had been firing nine to twelve round bursts six to nine rounds is ideal, but Krash was doing fine, because he tried to make that guy eat ever single one of the twelve round he fired at him. The man lumbered backwards, while bullets picked at his clothes and torso, his arms flailed wildly.

Another tried to jump into the cab of the truck to make their break, just as one of Derek's landed just outside the driver's door. The shithead was undeterred and regrettably, still undead. In my mind's eye, I saw Derek raise his weapon and say, "Let's see if you like this one better." *Thunk.*

Derek's next round seemed to go right through the driver's side window and into that shithead's ear. I shielded my goggle from the flash and thought to myself, *It well and truly sucks to be you today, you cocksucker!*

I got my three guardsmen on line again and moved them to within fifty meters of the remaining pair. I dropped behind a heap of scrap metal and sighted in on one of the two remaining. He'd had his arms full of metal scaffolding and shelving material that they were using for launchers and aiming devices. However when he saw his friend vaporize in the truck, he simply dropped all that he was carrying and in the next instant, I'd put two between his shoulder blades and he ceased to be a problem. My guardsmen on both sides of me were firing as though somebody might take away their ammo at any second. However, as near as I could tell, they hadn't hit anything.

The last man, ducked behind the pick-up, froze, looked about his feet. He looked to where Kevin and company were, then glanced my way. I yelled for him to surrender, thinking that maybe a prisoner might yield something. He had other ideas.

He suddenly stood up opened the truck, grabbed an AK and fired wildly at Kevin, Krash and Derek. A prisoner might've been nice, but I no longer felt like playing with him. I raised my rifle and drew a sight picture, then squeezed the trigger the same instant that Kevin and Krash did. The poor hapless bastard danced his final ballet for us just a second before collapsing.

There were no wounded and there were no blood trails. The only thing the left us was six Chinese rockets and some fuse. "Look. We heard you guys start shooting because even though they were gone, everybody in the valley here knows that the American's were out here killing the Taliban. They heard American M-4s and M-16s shooting and they Krash's RPK, our terps with their AK's also shooting, so everybody heard a different weapon shooting in response. Did they see them drive off? No! This is the best publicity and it's all free." The sad part of it all is, that I'm sure their unit was going to hang Bronze Stars on these jokers for no other reason than they went on this patrol. "Well, if we can find any heroes, we'll just fabricate them."

No matter. It's all good. We didn't get a prisoner, but we did get a body count.

* * * *

Tuesday, 24 August 2009
16:45
The body of a warlord from Shkin was discovered outside the FOB. This was highly unusual because these people had a great deal of influence in their areas. While the ANP didn't even go through the motions of pretending to investigate it, we were told the "apparent cause of death" was that he had been beaten in the head with a rock and then shot in the head. Clearly this was one creative suicide. The local ANP commander also said that this victim was once a very powerful member of the *Mujahedeen* during the Soviet Occupation. This body was later identified as Mustafa

"Stafa" Packm*allah*. Only that, no last name.

Later, a Major in the Cav OPCEN was on a tirade about the "apparent lack of intelligence from the intelligence section" and the failure of said section to connect the rocket attack with the as of yet, unidentified dead body. When asked, I simply stated, "While I have not seen the body, it is my understanding that there is no apparent evidence of rocket trauma." With that, I bid my farewell.

"Come back here," he bellowed.

I turned and took one step back. Only one.

"What's your name?" He demanded.

"Ya' don't know, do ya'?" With that, I turned and walked out, never looking back. There is a reason we don't wear name tags or rank. Yes, this *is* one of them.

* * * *

Wednesday, 25 August 2009
11:30

Tommy wasn't outside watching the street. It's not like he's any good when he *is* there watching the street. All he ever seems to bring with him is a pocket full of excuses. Perhaps that's not entirely justified. Which is the same as saying that most of the time, it *is* justified. My agent Marid, called me an hour ago and said he needed a meeting this morning. There was no time to get Tommy down here from Bagram, so I took my Interrogator friend and put him at the corner in a restaurant watching through the window, with a specific text code to send if we had company.

Again, we took side by side tables facing each other on different ends. We both diligently read our papers while Marid briefed me on what he knew.

"Jamal was able to get away from that big fight at Dowgar."

"I figured as much. His body never turned up among the dead."

"Jamal begged Ishmael to come to his rescue. His was the column coming from Jalallabad on the following day. After his column was slaughtered, he was convinced that Jamal had led him into a trap. Now he is trying to become Kwami's favorite commander. He is trying hard to impress him. He was trying to bring into our organization a powerful fighter from the *Mujahedeen*. However, he failed to convince him to come to us."

This was starting to come together. I tried to dig deeper. "What made this leader so powerful?"

"This is one of the warlords Karzai tried to co-opt into his government but did not want to go with him either. He still has a great deal of Russian tanks and most importantly, the petrol to run them. I have also heard that he even has SCUD missiles."

Well, this was shaping up nicely. "Okay, so Ishmaeli had him killed when he didn't join you?"

"No, he was quite angry to learn that his men killed him. I heard from one of them that Stafe came bearing gifts. He had brought them six rockets, and that he us to come over to him and he would be the boss, and not be a...sub...sub..." he searched for a word.

"Sub-commander?" I offered. *Six rockets: Three fired at the FOB, one abandoned at the scene, left two still at large.*

"No. Sub-servi-ent," he said it slow, as though he were sounding it out. He did not want to be subservient to either Ishmaeli or even Kwami. He wanted to be the main boss.

"Was this Stafa a local warlord?" I had thought all of them were disarmed, but it's possible they missed a few.

"No. I heard he was from far in the south by Kandahar, towards Pakistan. He keeps his Army in Pakistan so he does not have to give up his arms." Even before he said it, I knew it was coming. "I think he was from Shkin." I braced myself for another penetrating impact. *"Shkin! Why Shkin? Why does he have to be from Shkin?"* Now I just knew the Brigadier was going to send me down there.

"So, now what happens to his Army near Shkin now that he is gone?"

"I do not know. Perhaps his deputy Jamal Wazirdalah, takes charge and keeps them together. Perhaps not."

"Do you know where to find Wazirdalah?"

"Yes, I had to find him because now we have to approach him, since those men killed his leader. The directions to his place are folded up in this newspaper."

"Go ahead and set your paper down, then I'll do likewise and you pick mine up again. There's twenty thousand $400.00 USD, in here. That information about Jamal's rally was excellent stuff. You really produced for us. We won't forget that."

I sent down my paper, and took a sip of coffee, then busied my hands grabbing an ashtray and searching for a lighter. He set down his paper, and made a few notes. When he picked my paper back up, he said, "There is a lot of talk about trying to incorporate all of the fighters in the south under our organization. I think this is because Kwami wants to control all of the fighters in Western

Afghanistan and Eastern Pakistan. It is the only thing that makes sense."

It couldn't be just a power grab. That did make sense, but it just didn't answer all of the questions, like: Do they really have somebody in the White House? What has a shipping manager for a paper company got to do with this? Where do the Chinese come in? I knew that he would not be privy to these details, yet.

"What about this party that you want me to put on?"

"We want you to invite as much of your leadership as possible, and continue to plant little seeds of doubt where ever you can. You have already managed to cast suspicion on Jamal, with Ishmaeli. Later, we'll go to work on him, and at the same time bring you to the forefront of things. You've done very well. Outstanding. You can reach out to me anytime."

"Thank you. I will see you as soon as I know something more."

* * * *

Thursday, 26 August 2009
15:30

I arrived at Shkin, by another twin rotor CH-47. I asked for the assistance of another individual since I was going to meet with somebody who clearly resided in 'Indian Country'. Unfortunately, Tommy was busy trying to get a glimpse down the blouse of Moneypenny, Chris was out in the hinterlands on a tasking, and I was forced to take a volunteer from the Mehtar Lam conventional contingent. Which meant I was stuck with one of the three FOBBITs who accompanied us on our patrol from the other night? This man's name was Doug and he was from Las Vegas, Nevada. He was the Specialist who was an Infantryman. So, I felt a little better about that.

Doug was an unusual Specialist, which in the Army is only an E-4. He was thirty-five years old whereas most E-4s are about nineteen. Naturally, this brought a lot of questions from me.

"So, Doug, you're pretty old to be an E-4. How come?"

"Well, before I joined the NV National Guard, I was a Legal Clerk in the Naval Reserve."

"Why did you move over to the Army side of the house?"

"I wanted to see some action, get promoted. The usual."

"How long were you in the Naval Reserve?"

"Twelve years."

"You were only an E-4?"

"Promotions in the Navy are tough."

"So you joined the Infantry?"

"Well, I wanted to get promoted quickly and the quickest place for that is in the infantry." He totally missed the part about the promotions being so fast in the infantry because the casualties were so high. Despite what anybody says about the Infantry, eight percent of the total casualties still come from the grunts and ground pounders.

"You've been to the training though, right?"

"Well, no. I'm doing what my unit calls, OJT." Probably the reason he hadn't been promoted was that he never finished his OJT course.

This was great. He had no experience what so ever. He just jumped at the opportunity to work with Special Forces, and now he kind of like the idea of playing spy, wearing civilian clothes and carrying guns in a combat zone. This sucked nicely.

I told him some ground rules, "Okay, Doug; all you are going to do is drive for me. That's it. You don't use your weapon unless I tell you to—specifically who to shoot and when to shoot. Understood?"

"Yep."

"Look, this place gets hit probably three or four times a week. So brace yourself. However, keep in mind we have to find somebody and it has to be right after dark. This guy lives probably about thirty minutes from here. However, trying to find our way around these roads at night can be very difficult. Can you read a map?"

"Yeah, sure," he said.

I wasn't as confident.

* * * *

18:30

Doug and I were in the Tactical Operations Center TOC for Firebase Shkin, when five rockets impacted on the firebase. When one considers how small Shkin is, five rockets is a lot to soak up. Two of the Rockets had landed on the Chopper pad, and three had landed on the TOC. However, since rockets were such a frequent occurrence here, the TOC was reinforced with layer upon layer of concrete and sandbags. Since, Doug and I had no function in the TOC during a contact, they shoved us out to man a position on the wire and parapets.

18:35
Doug and I took up a position on the north wall, while the conventional force, a Rifle Company from the 82nd Airborne Division, was doing the very same thing. It was about this time, that the Taliban decided to make a ground attack on the firebase. Why? I'll never understand.

* * * *

18:45
Apparently several squads of Taliban were making some movement on towards the positions on the south wall. The noise of the return fire coming from the Rifle Company was rather impressive. Their machine-guns were working in controlled bursts, and all of their rifles exercised a lot of fire discipline. There was no action on any of the other three walls, and so infantrymen being infantrymen, wanted to get in on the fight. The one private who was standing next to Doug said, "I'd sure like to fire this." He lifted his M-203 grenade launcher to show what he was talking about. Then Doug immediately overstepped his bounds.

"Sure, go ahead," Doug told him.

The kid was amazed that he had just been given permission, by somebody in civilian clothes. Clearly this guy had to be somebody. Somebody like Delta, or maybe even...the CIA! Overjoyed, the kid asked for confirmation, "Really, Sir? It's okay?"

"Why not?" Came Doug's reply.

The kid popped in a 40mm Grenade and raised the weapon, "toook!" Off it went, "Kahhhh Rump!" came the reply from the distant impact.

"Hey Doug, maybe you don't want to be orchestrating this battle from the side that's *not* in contact with the enemy!" I told him.

I no sooner got the words our of my mouth when a parade of 82nd soldiers ran up to Doug, each with his own assigned weapon system, from squad sutomatic weapons, to machine-guns, to rocket launchers, to carbines—the whole plethora of infantry firepower was now on display for Doug, pending his approval.

Each of them asked, "Hey Sir, is this okay?"

"Sir, can I fire this?"

"What about this, Sir?"

"Sir, do you think it'd be alright if I fired this anti-tank rocket?"

Say Good Night

Doug gave them all blanket approval, "Sure guys. Have at it." Suddenly, the North wall of Shkin came alive with firepower. In the near total dark, I saw the lights of the Afghan National Police Barracks that was about 300 meters down the road. They built it there against our recommendation. We thought it was such a bad idea because it was entirely within our sector of fire and easily within range of every weapon. While the ANP had heard the firing from the South wall, it didn't really concern them too much, since they were north of the FOB, so they just went back inside. Now that they heard firing from the north wall, they thought somebody might come up behind them, so they poured outside to see what we were shooting at. When they saw nothing, they went back inside.

I grabbed Doug by the arm, "Doug, you don't want to do this! You can't tell these guys to blow off all their ammo! Their captain is trying to run a battle and you're just adding to the confusion."

"Oh, come on! It's no big deal. They just want to blow off some steam." At this moment, a young Specialist with a red Star Cluster flare this is an overhead flare used for visibility at night and shoots six to eight magnesium balls that burn white hot, "Hey Sir, would this be alright?"

Doug grabbed his shoulder and said, "Have a good time. Enjoy!"

Coincidentally, the fire on the south wall was slowly tapering off to nothing, either the Taliban lost their appetite for Shkin, or because they were now completely confused by this new attack on the north wall.

The kid, looking like he had just lifted a piece of candy from a store, scampered down the row of parapets and took the cap off of the flare, placed it on the bottom and struck it with his hand. However, he did not have a very strong arm because his strike caused his hand to tip and launch the flare almost straight out like a projectile. The cluster of magnesium balls shot straight out, and then glanced off of a rise about 200 meters in front of him. The balls all then sprang back up into the sky and continued on their journey into the windows of the ANP Barracks down the road. No less than five of the eight, small magnesium gifts made their presence known, by skipping into their open windows, perfectly!

The ANP poured out of their tiny barracks as it was now engulfed in flames. For our amusement, a Chinese fire drill took place before us. Live. The orange light completely lit the entire north wall's field of fire. If it wasn't painfully obvious before, it certainly was now, that there was not one enemy fighter out there, *anywhere*. The north wall was now completely engulfed in a pregnant pause. A hush seemed to descend upon the riflemen as they watched the ANP barracks burn, as the ANP were flapping blankets and rugs at the flames trying to put it out.

Then the Commander of the rifle company could be plainly heard, "What the fuck is going on here?"

I knew this was our moment to disappear. The Captain stood directly in front of me and bellowed, "What are you guys shoot at?"

* * * *

19:03
I yelled out, "Doug, look at the time. We've gotta get moving."

Looking very sheepish and humble, he simply turned and walked away. He was nothing like the grand master tactician I just saw at work a minute ago. Behind us, I heard a sergeant saying, "That guy from the CIA or whoever he was said we could fire."
"What guy?" Their commander was losing it.
"I don't know! Some guy!"

* * * *

19:45
It was now completely dark. It being Ramadan, I knew the man I was there to meet would be at home gorging himself after fasting all day. It was pretty tricky finding this place but my agent's directions were dead on the money. We parked in an open expanse about 300 meters behind his place which was on the outskirts of Shkin, which was on the Pakistani boarder, so for all I know, we actually may have been in Pakistan. We found a shallow draw and parked the hummer in there so as to keep it below the line of sight.

I told Doug, "You stay here with the vehicle, you park yourself right up here and you get in the prone. You stay there. You don't move. You don't do anything. If anybody comes, before you do, say, think, or shoot anything, he better be sticking the muzzle of a weapon in your face. Is this clear?"

"Yes," he replied timidly.

"Don't you ever pull a stunt like you did this evening. We have to get you out of there before those kids point you out to their Commander."

He simply and silently nodded.

I stepped out of the drawn and positioned Doug behind some rocks. Then I made my way to Jamal's mud hut, which was actually quite large by comparison to most in the area. I guess it pays to be the number two man in the largest Army for hire in Southeastern Afghanistan. I was going to try the direct approach.

I knocked on the door, and a woman came to the door, "Bali?"

I said simply, "Jamal."

She showed me in. Apparently she wasn't too worried about security, since he had about six other men with him at the dinner table. They were all stuffing their faces. I asked, "Does anybody here speak English?" Surprisingly, his wife did, as I thought, he was the one at the head of the table.

Through his wife, I said, "Jamal, maybe we want to discuss some business. Perhaps you don't want all of your associates to know what we are discussing."

He nodded, and stood up. With that he grabbed an AK-47 from the corner and we walked out of his dining room and into the street in front of his house. His wife came with us. I didn't like being that exposed so I took him around the corner of his house.

"Jamal, your boss has suffered a terrible beating and was murdered up near Jalallabad."

He was already nodding, through his wife, whose English was nothing short of amazing, he explained that some people from Jamal's organization have already tried to contact him about that and how they wanted him to join them.

"And your response was?"

"I am not so quick to jump into bed with the whore who has just killed my father," he said speaking metaphorically, "but I told them nothing."

"I would appreciate it if you kept it that way. Do not join them, because bad things happen to people who do." I didn't want to sound threatening because he might feel obligated to be defiant and then just join them out of spite. This would naturally be, counterproductive. Of course, I didn't want to put him on the payroll either, because that would require that I disarm him of tanks, anti-aircraft weapons, rockets, SCUDs and anything else he had, and I just wasn't prepared to do that now. That would be for another day.

"Yes, I have heard of such terrible things," He said this laughing, which left his wife confused. "I have heard of the slaughter of thousands of his Taliban fighters. I feel no loyalty to them.

They have punished Afghanistan worse than the Russians did. However, not all of my men feel the same way that I do. Not one of my lieutenants here with me tonight, but one who commands about a hundred soldiers, he may join them. He feels an obligation since he is a devote Muslim, and these people preach that they are the true faith of Islam."

"You don't believe this?"

"I believe that yesterday's leader is tomorrow's dog. However, I do not have the same control over my men that Stafa did. If my junior commander breaks from my band, I will call you." With that, I gave his wife my cell number and she wrote it out in Pashato.

"When you call that number, you should ask for a Colonel Binkus. Tell me, is it true that you have SCUDs?"

"Until yesterday, I wasn't sure, because Stafa kept them, even from me. Yes, I have now seen them and yes, we do have SCUDs, but we have no way to launch them. I believe that they are chemical warheads." I was becoming somewhat impressed with this 'warlords' savvy. He seemed to treat his wife with respect and he seemed knowledge about missiles and war heads. Not your typical goat herder turned soldier.

"They were very interested in my SCUDs, too. I might be persuaded to sell them." He was fishing for money. I can't say I blame him—we'd been spreading plenty of it around. He was going to have to find a source for it other than me.

"That would be fine with me. I would only ask you for a phone call when you do sell them."

"Such a phone call would be important to you. No?" Again he was fishing.

"Not terribly. I would think that you would be happy to make such a call after the way they treated Stafa. I would think that your loyalty and honor would compel you to make such a call." I was trying now to play on his honor. His wife yammered on in translation and I could tell by his facial expressions that I had played it just right. Mention his honor, don't question it, and certainly don't harangue on it.

His wife replied, "He says that you are right. He is willing to make such a call in light of what has befallen our leader.

To confirm matters, I said "So, I should get two phone calls from him. One when his junior lieutenant moves over to the Taliban, and one when he sells his SCUDs to the Taliban. Yes?"

He said simply, "Yes."

We shook hands, and I thanked his wife for her English,

"Where did you learn such perfect English?"

"At Oxford University, I was selected to attend from my school in Kabul. I was grateful it wasn't the American University in Gahgahstan.

* * * *

20:30
I found Doug exactly where I left him. We loaded up and we made our way back to the firebase at Shkin. We managed to slip in without raising any fanfare and went to sleep immediately.

* * * *

Friday, 27 August 2009
10:30
I left Doug in his room out of sight. I wouldn't even let him go to breakfast. I wanted to minimize his exposure so I just tossed him an MRE that I'd been hauling around for the last month. I won't let him put on civilian clothes either. I wanted him to look like Private Joe Snuffy, rifleman.

I went to the TOC because I needed one of their red lines, and called the J-2 Section to fill in the Brigadier. I was pleasantly surprised when Moneypenny answered the phone.

"Intelligence Section, Operations Desk. May I help you?"

"Hey, Moneypenny. It's Rick Burns."

"Oh! Master Sergeant, how are you?"

"I'm groovy. How are you?"

"I'm completely and totally hairless and exceptionally moist. I know the Brigadier will want to speak to you. Hold on..." She had given the word 'exceptionally' and added stress annunciation, and with that, she was gone.

"Well, good morning Sergeant Burns. What do you have for us today?"

"We have the cooperation of Stafa's heir-apparent and some confirmation regarding his SCUDs."

"Fine work. I'll see your report this evening?"

"Yes, Sir. This evening."

* * * *

11:30

Pilots have a long history of mercenary activities. Since World War I, American pilots flocked to join the French Air Force in droves at the war's outbreak. During World War II, American mercenary pilots became the Chinese Air Force by way of the Flying Tigers, and the Royal Air Force may not have weathered the Battle for Britain as well as they did, had it not been for their Eagle Squadron, of American mercenary pilots. In Afghanistan 2009, Canadian mercenary pilots...I give you Molsen Air! That's right, named for the beer. Strictly unarmed, non-combat transportation flights but critical none-the-less!

Another twin rotor CH-47 back to J-Bad followed by a Molsen flight to Mehtar Lam, putting me in at around 15:30 and completely severing Doug from my existence. *I hope.*

Chapter Seven

Period ending 9/20/09
Monday, 31 August 2009. 09:00

"Yes, Sergeant Burns, we've just had some developments in your neck of the woods, so to speak. It would appear that sometime during the night, somebody ambushed and blew up sixteen ISAF International Security Assistance Forces, fuel trucks as they were preparing to leave Pakistan for Kabul. It also appears that our friends Jamal and Ishmael are still angry about the pasting they took a couple of weeks ago," the Brigadier said, bringing me up to speed on the happenings of the previous night.

"So it would appear," I replied. "Do we know if this was suicide bombers or VBIEDs or rockets or what?"

"So far it appears to be the result of an attack involving multiple RPGs. At least that's what all indications look like now."

"Too bad we didn't get any early warning on this. Do you think that Marid has dried up?"

"Even with early warning, it's doubtful we would've been allowed to go into Pakistan to stop it. As for Marid drying up—it could be. It could also be that after that, they are now holding their cards much closer to the vest, in which case, we may have to do something about that."

"What do you have in mind?"

"Well, we planned for Marid to throw some sort of social function at his home and invite as many of the cell as he could muster. Perhaps we should move that date up to make it a Ramadan dinner, since they eat all night and will more than likely talk all night."

"Not a bad thought. Let's see about making that happen," The Brigadier was sounding weary which meant he was ready for the conversation to end. Fine with me.

"Yes, Sir." My next call went to Marid.

"I am telling you," he said. "I didn't hear about this until just now. It must be Jamal because nobody has better contacts and fighters in Pakistan than he does. However, he has been very suspicious of everybody since Dowgar. He hasn't been able to bring new fighters from Pakistan since then. That is why this attack occurred in Pakistan."

"Were they suicide bombers or was this a rocket attack?"

"I don't know. I will call you in a day or two when I have more information."

"Marid, if you are holding out on me, I got a ham sandwich here with your name on it! You better keep that in mind unless you plan on going to meet *Allah* with a mouthful of pork!"

"No! No! I'm not holding anything back. I don't see these people the same way anymore. I don't feel as though I owe them any loyalty. If I hear about it, I call you. Honest."

I believed him. Then I wondered how we might get some retribution for the drivers.

* * * *

Wednesday, 2 September 2009
10:28
Abdulah Lamentzor, The Director of Operations for the National Directorate of Security the Afghan NDS is equivalent to our CIA for Afghanistan was just leaving a conference with several other members of the National Command Authority. As he exited the building, the guard permanently assigned to his personal protection staff, got to door of his white Ford Excursion and held it open for him. He climbed in, and the bodyguard closed the door behind him and took the front seat passenger side.

A rather large bulky man approached the white SUV parked at the side of Ricket Street in downtown Mehtar Lam. He was wearing a light jacket that did little to hide the thirty pounds of C-4 explosives that he had in his suicide vest. As the lead vehicle pulled away from the curb to make a U-Turn in traffic, the second vehicle, carrying Abdul flashed on its turn signal and began to pull away from the curb. The large bulky man stepped up to the window and self-detonated.

* * * *

10:40
Mustafa, one of our terps called me and was barely intelligible because he was so frightened, or excited. Without being able to make much of his conversation, I grabbed Kevin who grabbed his aid bag and we headed down town. It was easy to find the blast

scene by just following the commotion in the streets. Several ambulances were pulling away from the scene, as we both arrived at 10:57. As the first ambulance pulled around the corner to take away some of the injured, small arms fire erupted down Eads Street with crossed over Ricket. Kevin was trying to reach Mustafa on the cell phone while we both readied our weapons and took off for Eads Street.

As the Ambulance made the turn, a line of gray metal bullet holes stitched it way across both back doors. The second ambulance was following the first through the same turn, and was eager to get out of the line of fire, but the pedestrians who were making forward movement impossible for the first, were holding the second ambulance squarely on the X.

Kevin put his cell phone away and we turned our attention to locating the gunmen. As the gunmen became more aggressive, the crowd thinned not wanting to get hit. Eventually, the two ambulances were allowed to proceed. Not without soaking up a lot of bullets first, however. We got to the corner, and heard the shots were coming from rather high up and not very far away. I glanced around the corner and saw one gunman on the far side of the street with an AK about 150 meters away on a second story fire escape, the same instant a second gunman opened up on our side of the street, also on a second story balcony. I told Kevin to take the one on the far side of the street while I get behind a parked car for cover and take care of the second gunman on our side. He nodded his approval.

I ran a couple of steps across the side walk to a parked Toyota, and sighted in on the second gunman. Kevin popped around the corner found the first gunman and nailed him the same time I found cover. The second gunman hearing the Kevin's M-4 was now scanning the street looking for the Americans. He was still trying to find a target when I put one through his chest and he dropped like a stone, where he never moved again. He didn't careen off of the rails, he didn't stagger around clutching his chest and then pitch over the rail in a dramatic head dive to the pavement. One second he was standing and firing, then the next millisecond, he wasn't.

* * * *

11:05
I no sooner stood up from behind the Toyota when I got a call

from Marid. He was speaking very quietly but I heard that he was in the crowd here somewhere because I could the same Sirens in the background from his phone.

"Are you aware of what just happened downtown?" He asked.

"Yeah, I'm down here now. Where are you?"

"I'm down Ricket Street just north of Eads and I am looking at Jamal. This was his attack and he is down here now to see the damage he has caused."

Although there was still plenty of pandemonium, the scene was secure, and the Director of the NDS was flying in to the area by helicopter. Kevin who was working the Afghan Pubic Protection Force APPF Regional Training Center RTC, at Mehtar Lam got the call on his cell phone from Colonel Shabir Itzik Afghan National Police at the RTC. He wanted him to go pick up the NDS Director and take him to the hospital where all of the casualties were being collected and treated.

Kevin caught my eye and I told Marid to hold on. Kevin filled me in and I tossed him the keys.

"Marid, does he know that you are out there?"

"No, he has no idea. It is a coincidence, sort of. I heard him say something last night about Ricket Street at 10:30, but I was not in the conversation so I had no idea what was going to happen. Had I known, I would've called you."

For the moment, I believed him. "It's okay, Marid. Does your phone have a camera on it?"

"Yes," came the reply.

"Okay, meet me at the northeast corner of Eids and Ricket." Within seconds, I saw him walking quickly and he slipped around the corner. I stepped up to him and asked him to point out Jamal in the crowd. As soon as he did, I recognized him.

"Marid, I'm going to go up and talk to him, and you make sure you get a bunch of pictures of the two of us together. I'm also going to hand him some money, you *must* get that picture!"

Marid nodded his understanding.

I slipped around the corner and meandered my way over to his side of the street. He stood there, not far off from the corner, a slight grin on his face, quite satisfied with the level of destruction which he had brought. Since I had nothing going that day, I was in uniform and all armored up. I had my M-4 slung in a non-threatening manner, and wondered if he had seen me drop his gunman like a hot rock. I was hoping he hadn't, as I slid along the side walk turning periodically to look over my shoulder and back down towards the blast scene. The Afghan medics were doing a decent job of bandaging and running. The ambulances flowed through at a steady pace. Since there was no small arms fire, I looked like just another American dog face trying to keep the street secure. At about 1 step per minute, I closed the distance.

When I was within an arms length, I looked at him and asked him, "Sir, do you know if the buses run through this piece of town?"

He looked at me wide eyed, as if to say 'why the hell is the American talking to me?' Then he shrugged his shoulders and yammered a sentence in Pashto.

I offered him a cigarette and then lit it for him, I asked him again about the bus. His English suddenly got better and he offered, "Yes, a bus...I think maybe I have seen a bus down here... maybe sometimes, but with this..." and he gave a sweep of his arms to indicate the pandemonium, "who knows? Why? Do you not have a ride?" Since I was in uniform, he knew I had a ride.

"Yes, I have a ride. I thought that I might hit the bazaar here this weekend." I then pulled a dollar from my pocket, it was only a single, but I folded it out and handed it to him, and hoped that Marid got that shot on his camera phone.

Then in a loud voice stepping away, I said, "Thanks for the information." It was more Kabuki theater.

* * * *

Thursday, 3 September 2009
01:30

Another two rockets impacted near the southwest corner of the firebase at Mehtar Lam. Most everybody slept through hardly hearing the impacts. All the communist made munitions are such junk. There is no mistaking the sound of American made versus Russian or Chinese manufacture.

I grabbed a terp and we took off the same launch site as last time. I really didn't think they'd be in the same place, after catching there last time. But one never knows. These guys can be pretty stupid sometimes. Unfortunately, I was right. They used a different site this time, and they had to be gone by the time we got to their old one.

Every night following this last rocket attack, a light show took place on the hills surrounding Mehtar Lam. One night to the north, the next to the south. The next night to the west, and then eventually east. There were no American forces involved in these attacks and it was determined to be Afghan War Lord vs. War Lord. This is what we call "Green on Green action," because we, the good guys, are the blue force. The enemy, regardless of who he is, is always the red force.

While officially, we were calling this 'green on green,' it was actually red on red. I am quite content to watch the HIG and the Taliban blast each other to pieces.

I thought that the HIG and the Taliban were slugging it out with each other for influence and control of the villages in Lahgman province. As long as they want to kill each other, far be it for me to interfere with domestic politics. I sat back and quietly enjoyed the light shows every night. Hopefully, after Ramadan, we could begin a real slug-fest in earnest!

Ramadan would be wrapping up fairly soon with the arrival of Eid, the three holiest days of the year for Muslims, which would be September 20-22.

* * * *

Saturday, 19 September 2009
01:00
"Alright Marid, we have microphones planted all throughout the house. All you have to do is get as many of the leadership to come to your place for Eid, as possible. Furthermore, you have to get them talking. Let them make as much small talk as they want. However, when they get down to business, just let them go. If Kwami comes, you have to find some moment to show him your little video of the two of us. Do you understand?"

"Yes, let them make casual conversation. When they get to business, let the conversations go, and if Kwami comes, I will show him my cell phone video. I understand."

With this accomplished, Tommy and I packed up and made tracks.

* * * *

Sunday, 20 September 2009
14:45
Tommy and I were sitting in a mud hut about 300 meters from Marid's house in J-Bad, with four terps, listening in on the four microphones that we had stashed throughout the house. We'd

been listening all morning, but nothing of substance had come across yet.

All through the noon feast, the talk concerned food, since they had all been fasting during daylight hours all through Ramadan. After their feast in the kitchen and dining room, everybody had adjourned to the living room and den area of the house. Small talk commenced.

* * * *

17:53
Several other members of the leadership began to arrive at the residence. Among them was Ishmael, and I hoped that he had brought lots of bad feelings for Jamal with him. It would be nice if we could nail Jamal's coffin shut tonight.

During this same period, most of Marid's family were saying their good-byes and leaving in two and threes.

* * * *

18:15
We heard the call to prayer going out from the prayer tower at the nearest Mosque on the north edge of J-Bad. They would all take part in another fifteen minutes of prayer, followed by another feast.

Almost as if on queue, the feast was ready right at the completion of prayer. Then, approximately ten minutes after that, Kwami arrived at the residence. Tommy and I looked at each other. It was promising to be a very nice night. Despite our initial excitement, we were very bored before their first meal was even half over. We fought to keep our eyes open during the after diner small talk.

* * * *

23:40
Marid could be heard talking to Kwami in one of his back rooms and the conversation sounded promising.

"Kwami, I have something very disturbing to show you. I took this video with my cell phone when I was in Mehtar Lam a few days ago, at the bombing down town.

Kwami's curiosity was peaked, one terp translated, "Let's see what you have there."

Marid's voice could be heard, "As you can see that is Jamal. And that man, I am told is the American spy master, a man named Colonel Binkus." I snickered to myself.

"What was that he gave him?" Kwami asked.

"Money," Marid answered.

"What did he say there?"

"He said, 'Thanks for the information'," Marid interpreted for him.

"This is very serious. We must not wait to deal with this problem. Our plans are too big to have him talking to the Americans. We must deal with him, tonight."

Jamaal could be heard on another microphone when Kwami came in and confronted him with the evidence against him.

"This man, yes, he is an American. But he asked me about a bus. That's all!"

"That is the American spy, Colonel Binkus! He doesn't need a bus!"

"This man was not a Colonel! He was a sergeant! With many stripes. No colonel!"

Marid confirmed my identity for Kwami, "No, I have it on good authority. The man is a spy. A colonel."

Kwami was through playing because there was a sudden commotion coming over the wire and we figured they must be taking Jamal into 'custody'. Tommy and I were desperate to see what happened next, and we weren't really set up to follow them if they decided to drive away. It's not like you can really follow anybody at night in Afghanistan anyways. There's no other vehicle traffic to hide in, in the outlying areas. Tommy and I took off on foot towards Marid's house and managed to get within a hundred meters in a matter of a couple minutes.

We saw clearly as four men held Jamal at the arms while he struggled against them. Kwami had in his hand a Russian Makarov pistol. There was much yammering going back and forth in Pashto, between the two of them, none of which we got. At one point, Jamal stopped struggling, stood up straight, yammered and spit at Kwami's feet.

This did it for Kwami. He stepped forward and placed the muzzle of the pistol to Jamal's head and without a syllable, pulled the trigger. The four men holding him let his body fall, then picked it up and threw it in the back seat of a car.

I turned to Tommy, "Well, I think we're done here."

"Yep. I'd say that worked out rather nicely."

"What is it you do here, again?"
Tommy replied, "Comic relief."
"Oh, yeah."

Chapter Eight

Week ending 9/26/09
Monday, 21 September 2009. 10:32

Tommy and I were in Brigadier Ferguson's office giving him a quick briefing of the developments at Marid's house.

He took out a long curved stemmed pipe and packed it with tobacco. This is something he did not do frequently. Smoke, that is. This was an indication that he liked what he heard.

The Brigadier sat in seat and snuggled down into it rather warmly, smugly. "I have to say gentlemen; I'm pretty pleased with this recent 'development'. In fact, I love it! I wish we could do this with all of them. Get them to feed on each other. Let's keep venturing down this path, shall we. See who else they'll get rid of for us. We should probably draft a target list for them. People we want out of the picture and people we think might be most susceptible to this kind of exploitation. Tommy, why don't you get started on that?"

Tommy nodded his acknowledgement in silence, as was his custom. Truth be told, I think the Brigadier intimidated him a little.

Now the Brigadier raised a finger, and pointed it squarely at me, "While he is doing that, I think I have something to keep you busy for a day or two. We've had a lot of unrest at the border with Pakistan near the Khyber Pass. ISAF and the UN, doesn't want a very big presence on our side of the boarder. But let's face it, the Pakistani's can't deal with the problem on their own. What I have in mind is some invisible support. Nobody will know you're there. In case you are caught, I won't either. You'll be best off saying you just got lost and they'll repatriate you within a couple of days."

"I'm not the only sniper in country. Not by a long shot, so to speak. In fact, I'm not even the best one for this. There are probably twenty-four ODAs in the eastern sector and any one of them could handle this. So, my question is: Why me?"

That's why I think you'll only be out there for a couple of days, while I take this proposal to the CJSOTF Commander and lobby for a rotating system of ODAs. All those ODA's are committed or otherwise engaged. You will be me putting a finger into a leaking dike. Get some sleep this afternoon, because I'm going to insert you tonight."

I truly did not envy the idea of going out by myself so far into the bad lands. There are just so many things that can go wrong. Even not taking the enemy into account. "Sir, there are two men in a sniper team...?" I asked leadingly.

"Yes, but it's easier to believe one man got lost than two. Besides, do you really want Tommy here as your spotter?" The Brigadier jabbed a thumb Tommy's way.

"Well, no. In fact, allow me to rephrase: Hell no! I was actually hoping you could find another sniper to go out with me."

"No. Not at this stage of the game anyways. Maybe if I had a few more weeks. You're not the only sniper in country, but you ARE the only sniper assigned to the J-2 Operations Section, which means you're the only sniper that I, specifically, ME, have. So, tag." The Brigadier reached out and slapped my shoulder. "You're it."

"This really isn't safe, Sir."

"All the more reason for you to be careful. Get started on the details, radios, COMSEC—Communications Security: This is equipment such as code books, cipher tables, radio fills for secure transmissions, etc.], frequencies, call signs, phase lines, code words, ciphers, supply—the usual." The Brigadier reached into his desk and took out two cigars.

He knew it was dangerous sending me out alone, so he mother hen-ed slightly telling me what COMSEC gear I would need, as if I haven't doing stuff like this for over twenty years, now he's trying to ease the bitter pill with a cigar. Well, I'll let him force one on me. Just every time he offers! I don't want him to think I'm a cheap date.

"Tommy," he said, "I'd invite you to join us, but this is a men's ritual." I thought to myself, *Wow! Good one Sir. Didn't see that one coming...*

* * * *

Monday, 23:45
The Brigadier's suggestion to sleep was a silly one. I had to jump on a flight to J-Bad that after noon, and link up with an ODA that was going out toward the boarder. We left J-Bad at 15:00 and set up in our RON Remain Over Night position at about 18:00.

There was no time for sleep.

The ODA's mission was to emplace cache points for me at chosen points along the boarder that would contain resupply items for me. Things like rations, water, radio batteries, ammunition, and a spare radio at one fixed point.

I was just now getting to put my head down for a rest. I left instructions for them to wake me at 04:00, so I could slip outside the perimeter and fade away. The team would wake up, break camp and pull out, *accidentally* leaving me behind.

* * * *

Tuesday, 22 September 2009
04:15
"Hey Rick, it's time, Buddy."

It was Eric Krampf and he gave my shoulder a slight shake. It was unnecessary, because I really had slept well at all. I was only able to get to that light sort of Alpha stage sleep, where you are constantly slipping in and out of consciousness, but never a really deep, restful sleep. It was always that way for me when I had a 'hard-time' a drop dead time, a time that had to be met, without fail. I sat up and Eric let me have a sip of his coffee.

I spent the next fifteen minutes packing up all of my gear for the next few days. I met up with Eric again, had a cup of MRE coffee. Yeah, it sucks. But what can you do? You deserve it. You signed the papers and took the oath. I shook hands with Eric and Ryan, and stepped off into the region known as the Swat Valley and the area around the Khyber Pass. The land of Kipling.

The entire was spent walking, resting, making coffee and doing my best to stay out of sight. This meant slow stealthy movement. At some point in the early afternoon, I figured that I must've passed into Pakistan, because I paused outside a small village and saw a Pakistani Boarder Militia vehicle drive up and talk to several villagers.

I remembered from my last tour that the Boarder Militia is an irregular civilian defense force consisting of people recruited from the local areas. The Pakistani Border police had a reputation for being much more professional I think it's important here to remember that when I say that they are more professional, all thinks are relative. Since these Militiamen are locals, I thought it would be a very good thing to see who they are talking to, since I thought that most of the reason Pakistan can't get a handle on their Taliban problem is because of these asshole providing cover and medical support for Al Qaeda, even against the Pakistani Army. President Musharif wanted to disband them before he left office, but now...

I watched and made a mental note of who they spoke to in the village. After an hour, the militia-men left with no new passengers. I moved on. I wanted to get to a good position close to one of the boarder's customs inspections points before the sun went down.

* * * *

Tuesday, 16:30
I found a decent hide position that was within 700 meters of the northern most check point coming out of the Khyber Pass. I did some very minimal preparations and improvements to the position, filled a few sandbags, shifted some logs and rocks to provide cover and concealment. I used and entrenching tool to scrape out the bottom of the position and build up a slight parapet. The hide position had the best field of view of the target area and almost no dead space space which can not be covered by direct fire weapons, to speak of. The position didn't have a very good field of fire to the rear of my target area, but so be it. I have my M-4 for the closer fight, and my Barrette for when it's up close and personal. I took the time to string some Claymore mines out to my flanks and rear and string a few hand grenades on trip wires.

* * * *

Tuesday, 20:30
I went to sleep early to try and make up for the deficit that I was operating in.

* * * *

Saturday, 26 September 2009
04:00
The last several attacks had taken place in the very early morning hours, so I woke myself up at 03:00 every morning to watch for anybody moving in or watching from another position. I used a thermal sight to illuminate anybody or anything with a pulse in the dark. Now, I may have hit pay dirt.

Through the sight, I clearly saw the forms of two individuals and they moved down the side of the ridge line on the opposite side of the highway from me, approximately 1100 meters away. I watched them move cautiously and deliberately down the ridge to a point where they were about 900 meters from me, where they stopped and seemed to set up their own observation post. They just squatted and watched the checkpoint below. The checkpoint was clearly visible, bathed in a pool of huge standing tower lights.

Four Pakistani Border policemen manned the checkpoint below, with two, wheeled armored vehicle and a squad of Pakistani Army soldier's standing by for security. All totaled out to about a dozen men armed with small arms and maybe a light machine-gun.

Shortly before sun-up, they withdrew without any further activity or aggression. It seemed worth hanging around another day or so, just to see what developed.

* * * *

Sunday, 27 September 2009
03:35
Little more than a half hour into my early watch, I was beginning to think that I was wasting everybody's time I saw three appear over the rise on the ridge opposite from me. Seconds later, another four appeared and followed.

Ten minutes later, five more men appeared over the ridge and walked down towards the other seven. Finally, nearing 04:00, the final four arrived over the ridge and came together with the rest of their cabal. It was clear they were going to do a lot more than watch today. Through the thermal slight I saw them preparing for an ambush: Checking weapons, briefing other soldiers, etcetera.

Eventually, they all moved down toward the road at the bottom of the valley, finally coming to a stop at a position about 200 meters from the Khyber Road which passed through the Checkpoint. Here, one broke off from the group and returned back up over the ridge out of sight. Leaving fifteen at the valley floor. They had roughly two hours before sunrise. I also noticed that they didn't put out any security to their flanks, these are little one or two man posts a little further out from the main elements to keep from being surprised on your flanks.

About thirty minutes later, the one I saw break off and leave, appeared again, at the summit of the bluff overlooking the checkpoint and a turn in the road. I suddenly realized that I was on the wrong side of the road if I had hopes of developing any new information. However, I was on the right side of the road, if I just wanted to kill them all. What to do? I decided that since I was still in the intelligence business, it was probably best to at least try to gather some actionable intelligence. Although, I got the impression from the Brigadier that he was not too concerned about any new 'collection'.

I slung the sniper rifle across my back. I was now well within range of their weapons , and that would mean I'd have to acquire and engage targets much faster and much closer, making the sniper rifle and the scope impractical. I brought up my M-4 and left my hide, and began a descent of the slope I was located on, and prepared to cross the Khyber Pass road, to put myself on the side as the ambush. This could be dangerous if the Pakistani Border police don't exercise due caution.

* * * *

Sunday, 04:45

I crossed the road about a hundred meters to the west of the ambush and on the other side of a slight bend. Once on the same side of the road, I moved up towards the ambush point. I know that fifteen to one are some tall odds, but that element of surprise can go a very long way.

I moved forward and closed the distance on their left flank. They would pay for their mistake when they didn't put security out.

* * * *

Sunday, 05:50
Start of Action.

Now, less than fifty meters away from the ambush, a low loud whine and growl could be heard coming from deeper inside the pass. Deeper inside of Pakistan. A few seconds later, from around a bend in the pass, came a convoy of ten fuel trucks. I could make out the ISAF placards on the trucks.

In the meantime, I had no less than fifteen shitheads to my front. They were spread out in front of me in a row, or column. I was at the western most point of their positions as they spread toward the east. If I walked straight forward, I could step on every single one of them, except the man on the bluff overlooking the

Police Checkpoint. I glanced up at him, silhouetted nicely with the light from a rising sun, I saw him raise an RPG to his shoulder. I watched my opposite numbers as they pressed themselves lower into the ground, and brought stocks up to shoulders.

As soon as the first truck came to a stop at the checkpoint, the last had just rounded the bend in the highway leading from the pass. Gray tones of the early morning light provided a very limited view of the vehicles in their 'kill zone,' still in the shadows of the mountains.

Suddenly, the man on the summit with the RPG initiated the action, by sending a rocket down into the last fuel truck in the pass. Huge billowing balls orange flames laced with black ribbons of petroleum soot rolled skyward and lit the valley floor as though it were mid-afternoon. Immediately after that, the man nearest my position began to engage the police checkpoint with his RPK, belt-fed Russian machine-gun.

I watched as one Pakistani Boarder cop exited the armored personnel carrier, APC, at the checkpoint and was then cut down by the RPK gunner as he laid a stitch of bullets along the vehicle and then headed for the checkpoint again. The RPG gunner had loaded a second rocket and fired it into the APC. It penetrated the top of the vehicle where the armor skin is thinnest. The vehicle lurched and leaped off of the ground briefly, but that was it. Anybody still inside was now most likely dead.

I watched as all of the men in the ambush party began to creep forward, towards the vehicles on the road. The RPK gunner was stopped. Having no assistant gunner, he tried desperately to load another belt of ammunition as I approached him.

The boarder cop manning the checkpoint had been the first to go, and now those that were contained inside the small barracks were trying to obtain some firing position. After seeing four more go down, I decided to put a stop to things. Technically speaking, this was not my fight. I was in Pakistan. My fight was about 400 meters behind me.

When I was a few yards from the machine-gunner, he pulled the charging handle back on his machine-gun, finally getting the belt seated. He noticed me and gave me a quick look, which I repaid him with a quick burst of my M-4, I caught him at his right hip and stitched him up to his left shoulder. He spun around and dove face first into the ground.

For a nanosecond, I thought about taking the belt-fed RPK, but decided to stick with the M-4. It would be faster and easier to reload. With the machine-gun out of the picture, I immediately took off at a run toward the next man in line who was approaching a rock, but never made it. He never saw me as I came up slightly behind him. I took the rock he was going for, just as another RPG rocket struck the Pakistani barracks.

Bracing myself against the rock, I took careful aim at the RPG gunner about 300 meters away. He was trying to load his fourth rocket when my bullet struck him somewhere in his torso. He spun to his left and fell from sight, never to be seen again.

In the same breath, I brought my weapon back down to engage the next man in line who was only about twenty-five meters away. At the sound of my different M-4 carbine, he turned, looked, and with a little assistance from me, he dropped stone dead for his troubles. On to the next.

Coming up on his four o'clock position, fifty meters away. Aimmm...steady...two shots, center of his back. Good! On to the next. There he is.... I killed the next one much the same way as I had the last. I was now consistently coming up on everybody's four o'clock.

Now I was no longer sure how many I had killed, or how many were left in front of me. Furthermore, the shit heads now knew I was here, so my element of surprise was going to dwindle rapidly. I picked up my pace and engaged one more, who seemed to be torn between the rock he'd just left and the road which held his objective. He brought his weapon to bear on me but wasn't fast enough on the trigger.

I grabbed another magazine and brought it up to my weapon, with the same hand, I took the nearly empty magazine and replaced it in less than a second. Re-load when you can, not when you have to. I put the empty in my pants cargo pocket. With that done, I took off at a run again. I wanted to get all the way to the last man in the next few seconds.

There! Three of them! Set up so sweetly! Now, aimmm...a few short bursts...one more burst. No, one more. Now reload! On to the next.

I saw a cluster of four more shitheads stop in the middle of their rush, while they took a second to size me up. They were all packaged nicely in a little five meter cluster. A typical fatal mistake of the amateur soldier. I engaged them with a series of both short and prolonged bursts. A gray mist rose up from the ground as an endless fusillade of bullets pounded the earth around them.

I watched as they fell like rag dolls. *There's no time to admire your handy work! Get Busy! Stay focused! On to the next. There he is!* I moved from bush to rock and from rock to bush and back to bushes again. Every time I stopped, I engaged a target.

I had the hood of my ghillie suit off and resting on my shoulders. I couldn't really ignore what had happened behind me because I wasn't really sure how many, if any of them were actually dead. I didn't want to be surprised myself by a wounded and angry shithead.

Keep your eye on the ball! What's behind me? How many more do I have in front of me? What am I doing? You're reloading, Stupid! Reload when you can, not when you have to! Do it now! There you go! Now you've got a full magazine again. But you still have a full plate you idiot! You bit off more than you can chew here! Shut the fuck up, and get on with the task at hand. Next man? Where are you? Where is he? There! Good! Another one down.

Now the few remaining boarder cops were consolidating their numbers. All three or four of them who were still alive. This was a problem because they had no idea who I was. I wasn't wearing anything approaching one of their uniforms and was therefore, as legitimate a target as anything else moving about to their front.

I was amazed as I now had only five more remaining in front of me. One of them looked back at me, as I raised my weapon to my shoulder. He said something to the other four. He slowly raised one hand. The remainder froze, watching his every move, waiting to see what happened next. He started to lay his weapon down and said in pigeon English, "Sooorender…?"

Still looking down the sights, I gestured with my left hand, and said, "Okay, put your weapons down on the ground." This was what I was afraid of really. I couldn't really afford to take these guys prisoner. *So, now what? Kill 'em?*

The shit head that stood closest to the Pigeon English boy, suddenly got a scowl on his face and yelled at me. I didn't have the time or patience to deal with him, so I put two in his brain case, right between his eyes. *Blaam. Blaam!* He crumpled like the piece of shit that he was. Everybody else sat up and took notice. Suddenly, if they didn't speak English, they were a brand new student of the language. Everybody was falling all over each other trying to impress me with how important they are or how much they know.

I told them all to shut up. Knowing it wouldn't be long before the border police closed in on me, I asked pointed questions:

"What were you guys after today?"

"We were to take all of the fuel trucks that we could get, to a point southeast of Shkin, in Pakistan."

"Where? Specifically?"

"I don't know. I was supposed to call him when I got to Shkin."

"Who's your contact? Write down the number you were to reach him at," and I tossed him my note book. He did as he was told.

"Why? Who needs the fuel so bad?"

"It is for Mohamed Mullah Khan a new player I had never heard of before. He has a thousand tanks and he needs the petrol…very…hmmm? Very bad?"

"Alright, if you guys want to live, you'll keep your mouths shut and this conversation never took place. Do you understand?"

They all shook their heads. "Here is my Roschan phone number…" and I read it off for them. Two of them wrote it down once I tossed them a pen.

"The next time you hear something regarding those tanks, you call me. Right?"

Again, they all shook there heads.

"You can ask your friend here," I said point to their buddy with the attitude who was now assuming room temperature. "Ask him how much I patience I have for fools. If you tell your leaders we talked, they won't believe you that you didn't give up some information to me and they'll kill you. You need to tell them that the border police were better prepared than you anticipated. That they got the better of you today."

Pidgin English said, "You should know, that Kwami has a forger at work on many pages of a document. I don't know what the document is, but it is in Chinese and in English. That is all I know."

"Okay, when you call me, you're Pigeon," I said pointing to him and then the other two. "You are Dove, and you are Crow." They all nodded their understanding and kept my pen while they made more notes.

A burst of AK fire raked overhead from the border police told us that now felt that with the sudden drop in fire, they were now the victors in this engagement. That was fine with me. I looked at the mess that was once the vehicle checkpoint.

"You guys leave your weapons there, and you go that way *east*, give me my pen. You don't want to have to explain why you have it. We'll talk soon."

****

Sunday, 06:07
End of Action.
With that, they turned and fled, and I turned and disappeared into the hills surrounding the Khyber Pass.

****

15:15
I was well into Afghanistan and about 300 meters from a Karez. These are underground rivers and canals that were used at one time to irrigate farmer fields. They're usually good watering holes and this karez was a known point for me. I'd seen it on the way out and knew this to be a good spot to refill my canteens.

However, here I now saw no less than twenty people come piling out of the slight dip in the earth. They were all dressed in typical Haji garb with *shamags* and man-dresses. They split into two separate groups and quickly scattered throughout the desert.

I watched the watering point for about thirty minutes and saw no movement whatsoever. I approached very cautiously using maximum stealth. I was moving so slowly and light on my toes, that it probably took me twenty minutes to cover the last twenty-five meters.

When I got to the watering hole, I found nobody else there. I also found the strangest formation of equipment. On the floor of the wadi that led to the karez, lay two separate and distinct formations of equipment. Four rows of rucksacks, shoulder sacks, ammunition vests and belts, and relatively new AK-74s of Chinese manufacture. Some of the first I'd ever seen. All this personal military equipment was lined up in four rows of five, with one in the center totaling twenty one soldiers.

The fact that I had already burned a great deal of time in my cautious approach to this sight put me up against the clock. The fact that they had not posted an equipment guard, led me to believe that they booby trapped their equipment. It also told me they did not plan to be gone long. All of which meant that I could not do anything more than really look them over hard and snap a few pictures with the disposable 35mm camera that I carried with me.

Standing back and looking at this formation of equipment, made my hair stand on end. To see more than twenty stacks of military equipment of another nation who was uncertain, stacked and dressed right, all covered down as though in Basic Training, sent a message of highly disciplined troops. Two squads of ten of them each, operating in our area? Just who the hell were they? What could their mission be? Well, I guess that all depends on who they are? It was all a little concerning.

No matter, I had a chopper to meet. I used a branch to cover my foot prints as best as possible. Then after refilling my canteens, I moved on to my Pick-up Zone.

* * * *

Monday, 28 September 2009
10:10
Brigadier Ferguson sat looking out the window, pipe clenched in his teeth, deep in thought. "So, we have no idea where this armor is right now, but we do have the contact's phone number?"

"Yes, Sir."

"Well, this was a very unexpected surprise, Rick. I'm quite pleased." He said nothing of the twelve or more people I had just killed. Perhaps he didn't know about those details? Perhaps he really had no more idea of what happens out there, than what I tell him? The Pakistani Police may not have told anybody that they took such a pasting? Perhaps it's better this way? Perhaps it's best not to dwell on such matters? Apparently, I was still 'Rick'.

"Make no mistake Rick, I'm always glad to see you. When will you have fresh intelligence for me, too? Well, let's admit it, sometimes it better to see you than others. No offense, of course."

"None taken." I did my best to look stoic. Impassive.

"Well, let's see what comes from that phone number, and then we'll have to see about confirming whatever information comes from that source." I knew what he meant. Once a piece of intelligence has been 'cultivated' from one source, it should be confirmed by using another discipline or source before it becomes "actionable."

"Sir, I assume that you've seen the pictures of the stray equipment that I found out there. Any thoughts?"

I was also curious as to the discovery of a new unit on the battlefield and how we were going to proceed on the issue. He withdrew the pipe from his teeth and said, "Yes, that certainly is a very big surprise and a very curious development. I think we'll tread lightly and keep this one close to the vest for awhile, until we receive some addition intelligence from other sources. You understand, of course. We'll pass it up the line, but we don't mention it beyond these walls. Not yet anyways. Right?"

"Right, Sir."

He was just thinking out loud. He knew I wasn't stupid on this point.

Without another word, I left his office and made my way to the break room and the coffee pot contained therein.

I felt her hand on my forearm as brought the cup of coffee from the counter, I turned and looked into her bright blue eyes and brilliant smile, which were such a contrast to her now dark bronze complexion. Apparently, she'd been doing a lot of sunbathing. "Hi Moneypenny. Can I buy you 'a brew?'"

"No, I'm afraid I only have another minute or so, before the Monday morning 'intel dump,' re-commences. I just wanted to say 'hello,' and to let you know that I've been thinking about you a great deal lately."

"Why would that be?"

She looked incredibly uncomfortable. Truth be told, I think she was worried; perhaps even worried about me. However, my thought was, *she liked to use sex as a defense mechanism.* A way of deflecting from serious topics: Emotional moments, or matters of the heart. She suddenly got a very wry, sinister smile.

"Well, let's just say that it...that it involves... Well, it involves... C cell batteries."

"Why Moneypenny, I'm sure I don't know what you mean."

"How unfortunate for you that is, then. Perhaps, if you were to stop by my hootch this afternoon, I might show you..." She smiled, turned and left. When she got to the door, she stopped, turned and again smiled so beautifully, gave me a wave of her fingers and said, "Toodles."

* * * *

16:00

I knocked on the door to Moneypenny's 'hootch' to get no answer. I suspected that she would be on the roof again, sunbathing. I climbed the ladder reluctantly, knowing that once again, I was climbing into the belly of the beast. Now, the beast was anxious for retribution.

As I looked out over the roof of the man-can, to see her on her folding cot, sunning herself on the roof. I really had no excuse for coming up here, so I knew that I was in for it. But then again, I was sure that I deserved it. Alright Richard, go take your beating...

"Moneypenny, ahoy..." She was lying on her stomach and I saw her raise her head and wave me up to the roof. I walked closer and she lowered her sunglasses and waited for her eyes to adjust.

"Well Richard, what brings you around here?" she said with a curious tone.

"To be honest Moneypenny, the last time I was here, I guess that I was rather mean to you. I mean, leaving you in such...how did you say it? Mood?"

Moneypenny nodded, "For leaving you in such a mood."

"Well, you should be sorry. That was a perfectly awful thing to do to me."

I raised a finger, "Who did what to whom?"

She shook her head, "Never mind. I don't want to get into a down in the weeds discussion over culpability. I'll just accept your apology and we'll be done with it." I nodded and extended my hand to shake, in forgiveness, be friends again.

Moneypenny cocked her head slightly to one side while she looked at me quizzically, as though she were trying to determine just how serious I was. I was very serious. We held hands for a very long time, looking into each other's eyes. Not a word was spoken. There was really nothing to say.

Finally, I simply said, "Moneypenny, next time."

She stood and gave me a wonderful view of that lean, sculpted bronze body of hers. No Union Jack bikini today. This one was a mere collection of three small triangles. The one covering her lower lips could not have been more than two inches at its widest, while the triangles covering her nipples were hardly much bigger. *Exquisite! Never mind Richard, it's time to go.*

Moneypenny, on the other hand, had other ideas. I turned toward the ladder, "Oh, Richard. Before you go, it's time for me to turn over, and since you did such a wonderful job of putting lotion on my back. I hope you will do my front for me, pleeease..."

I turned back and at that moment, I saw Moneypenny holding the bottle of lotion sideways at shoulder. She gave it a squeeze launching a long stream of white lotion on to her own breasts, and said "Oooppss..."

How conniving. She knew exactly what she was doing. She also knew this visual would keep me rooted in place like an oak. My eyes were locked on to he beautiful bronze breasts that were doing their level best to burst from that bikini top. Her skin was shiny and wet with perspiration and that long stream of lotion shot diagonally across the tops of her breasts and was now running down the slops and valleys in streaks, mingling with the rivulets of sweat forming on her skin, I watched as it flowed down the valley of her cleavage and I followed the line of travel to the peaks of those breasts confined within cups that seemed just barely high enough to cover her nipples, the triangles were so small I could see the underside of her breasts and almost all of the sides. I stared on, knowing that at any second, I might be struck blind.

I treated my eyes to those flat toned abs of hers, down to her taunt tummy and the sweeping spread of those curvaceous hips, I stopped my eyes and tried to bring them back to her face. To my credit, I did for a second. Then I found myself fixed again upon the globs of white, slowly streaking their way down her breasts. You know exactly what it looked like. I looked at my feet and shook my head.

Moneypenny repeated, "Pllleeezzzeee..."

"You win Moneypenny. I should've known better than to cross blades in this arena with a woman, especially you. You are the undisputed Master of Sexual Frustration. I know when I've been beat."

In a gratuitous display of dancing on her opponent's grave, she fired another shot of lotion on to those sculpted abs, "Won't you just rub it into my stomach?" She began working the lotion in slow, low circles; down towards the top line of her bikini bottom, which was already so wet and cut so low, I would've known had she not shaven that day.

I raised my hands in clear and obvious surrender, then I turned and walked to the ladder, making sure to never look back at her. I heard say once more, "Please, Richard...?"

I know that there probably aren't too many men in Bagram who would've passed up the opportunity that I'd just had. But! My marriage is still in tact!

Chapter Nine

Week ending 10/6/09
1 October 2009. 09:38, Bagram

My Roshan phone rang and I didn't recognize the number, but I did recognize the Pakistan Country Code of 72 on the caller ID.

"Bali?" I said into the mouthpiece.

"Hello? Am I speaking to Mister Binkus?"

"Yes, you are. Who am I speaking to?"

"This is your very good friend, Jeff."

I didn't recognize his voice because I had barely talked to him, but it was Mustafa Organahyi, the shipping manager from the Wazirk Paper Company in Pakistan. Before we had parted ways after that afternoon in the compound back in August, I assigned him the source name "Jeff".

"Well, Jeff. What a nice surprise! I was beginning to think you'd forgotten about me. What's the reason for this call?"

"I would not forget you. I am calling to tell you that I am sending several rolls of paper to meet with the engraver by Shkin. Trust me. This is very important. You will be interested in this delivery. I have been told that he will have some plates of importance and a secret Chinese document from the forger. That is all I have been told, 'the secret document' and the 'plates of importance'. I will be delivering that order on Wednesday of next week." I looked at a calendar that was the seventh, so I had a little time to work with.

"Where is the engraver coming from? Do you know?"

"I believe he is Chechnya, but I think he will be coming from Karachi."

"But your delivery is coming from Islamabad and going to meet him at Shkin?"

"Yes, they will be meeting up with a group of fighters coming over from Pakistan, and they will ride with the trucks carrying the paper. I have been told that there are very many fighters. As many as five hundred fighters, and a hundred tanks."

"Five hundred? Really? With tanks?"

"I don't know. Because they have had a great many problems recruiting here."

"Why Shkin?"

"I heard they have a printing press near Kandahar, and it is the best crossing point from Karachi."

"Where are you supposed to make the delivery?"

"It will be a small abandoned house on a tribal road I know these and they are little more than dirt trails, exactly 1.2 kilometers from the first northern trail off of the Pakistan border crossing road. There is no address. The house is on the East side of the trail. It is a very small house of just two rooms."

"Thank you, Jeff. I look forward to hearing from you again."

I made my way down to the Brigadier's office and passed Moneypenny in the hall and I said "Hi" in passing. I sensed that she wanted to stop me and chat for a bit, but I was having none of it. As much as I would love to discuss Moneypenny's grooming habits, at this point in my tour, I needed no such aggravation.

I saw that the door was open. I saw the Brigadier look up as I approached, he smiled large and gave me a wave to come in. I silently hoped that he didn't have anything else for me than had already landed in my lap this morning.

"Sir, I just heard from one of the sources I cultivated back in August. It would appear that tree is beginning to bear fruit."

"Well, what news did he have for us?"

"He said that we have an engraver that is supposed to meet a delivery of paper on the 7th, along with some secret Chinese documents next week."

"The Chinese, the Paper and an Engraver. I expect that I should get on the phone again to your Secret Service."

"What makes you think it's only American Currency they are going to duplicate?"

"Good Point. I'll get on the phone to the Royal Treasury as well. Perhaps you should see what your FBI friend has to say about it." He didn't say as much, but he wanted me to refer this matter to the FBI.

"Yes, Sir. Is there anything else?" I asked, hoping there wasn't.

"No. Well, yes. Your friend Sergeant Anderson has been hanging around the PX with nothing to do. Take him with you."

"Why does he have to be my friend? Why do I always get stuck taking Tommy?"

"I've told you: Nobody else will have him."

* * * *

14:30
Down to the Bagram Beanery where I found Liz sitting at a Table. A Triple shot of espresso please, and I take it over to Liz. Unfortunately, Tommy showed up about five minutes later. Perhaps it was a blessing that Tommy showed up because he puts a damper on whatever you are feeling at that moment. Liz was almost pretty enough to make me forget I was married. Almost! Now, with Tommy here, it would be like drinking espresso make from Salt Peter.

"Okay, Liz. This is what I got," I said as I slipped her a copy of the report I typed up as a result of this source contact.

"Thanks. I'll give it a read when I get back to the office. Are we going out soon?"

"Well, it looks like you might get your wish. By the way, you remember Not-So-Special Agent Anderson?"

"Who? Oh, Yeah. Hi."

"Hi."

"Call me when you've had a chance to digest that," I said and we continued to make small talk for the next twenty minutes.

* * * *

18:00
"Hey Rick, its Liz. I've read your report, and I made a call to Quantico. They said I have to refrain from any active combat, but they also said I can go with you to take custody of any evidence which may be seized in connection with this matter."

"'Any active combat?' as opposed to the mundane, sedimentary combat? Okay, we'll meet up with the Brigadier tomorrow in his office and discuss a course of action. However, I think you should pack a bag. I think you'll be going with me."

"Goodie, goodie gum drops!"

I couldn't believe she really said it.

* * * *

2 October 2009
09:15
Brigadier Ferguson asked, "What did the Secret Service have to say when you talked to them?"

"That they will be content to have the FBI seize the evidence of a case of an obvious Secret Service preview and then receive the evidence on a 'controlled transfer'."

Looking at Liz now, "I don't like sending civilians out on combat operations and this is not an adventure park. I'm going to let you go on this one, because I know Rick, here," he gave me a nod of his head. "He knows his way around the place and through this business plus he is a damned good field operator. I know he'll bring you back alright. If he does nothing else good, the one thing nobody can dispute is, as you Americans say. He brings home the goods! I don't like the idea of doubling his burden in playing nursemaid to a civilian. I don't have to play these sorts of games, so I don't. If Rick doesn't feel you're up to it, then you don't go. That's final.

"Now, I'm going to put together a tasking for a Special Forces ODA to take down this delivery. It's been refused." Now he was talking to me directly, " I want you to go in and get your hands on the plates and these mysterious secret Chinese documents which this engraver is to bring."

"What does the Royal Treasury have to say?"

"We don't have the same chain of custody requirements that you do. But, they are sending a representative down here, I'm not sure why."

So, it has been said, so it will be done.

"Now, about that ODA: The CJSOTF has no desire to deploy an ODA so close to the Pakistan border. You may recall that such thinks often produce questionable results." I thought he was making reference to an incident in 2003 where a platoon from an unknown SEAL Team It may have been Team 4, but then again, it may not have been, not that I'm saying this ever occurred, accidentally pursued a company of Pakistani Border Militia well into Pakistan and had them cornered inside of a mud hut for the better part of a day, before the error was realized. *Ooops!*

The Brigadier continued, "Instead, all they are willing to give me are two other snipers. One from 22 SAS Special Air Service, and one from the Royal Marines, SBS Special Boat Squadron: Equivalent to our U.S. Navy SEALs. Actually, I believe you already know them."

He was half wrong, I only knew the Royal Marine from previous work experience. The SASman was a Captain who'd been promoted up from the ranks. In the British Military, once a Senior Noncommissioned has reached all of the enlisted and Sr. NCO pay grades, his next promotion is to Captain it's worth noting here, that despite their rank, these officers are never accepted as

"Proper Officers". This promotion system from enlisted to officer, is unheard of in the U.S. Military.

This was also the SAS's way of taking command of this operation. By providing the Officer in charge...

* * * *

6 October 2009
21:00, Shkin

It was an incredibly dark night. There was heavy cloud cover so there was no illumination. The three of us all slipped out of the wire at FOB Shkin. Liz had been enthusiastic and eager to learn during the preceding two days of rehearsals and immediate action drills. My little patrol consisted of Liz, myself, Not-So-Special Agent Anderson and a 'gentleman' from the Royal Treasury, by the name of Howell. I took to calling him Thurston.

The SAS Captain, a guy by the name of Muglesworth, and was consequently called Mugsy, with his co-conspirator from the SBS, a Staff Sergeant by the name of Howser, aka, Louie, left out at about 08:00 this morning to get eyes on the target area a good twenty-four hours in advance. Both were snipers with considerably more experience than I had so I didn't have any qualms about letting them guide us into the target area.

* * * *

7 October 2009
00:25

We were crossing a small wadi, when suddenly a Hilux pickup truck rounded a bend in the dried up river bed. We all scrambled back to the wall of bank we had just left. We all stayed plastered against the steepest wall we could find. However, our luck was running dry when the two vehicle convoy came to a stop just 75 meters away and the wadi where we were standing was suddenly flooded with dozens of Al Qaeda fighters.

Liz reached up an pulled my ear down towards her mouth, "Do you think we are going to make it out of here?"

I whispered back, "Duuuhhh. I ain't gettin' planted here."

Thurston started to whisper something but he was too far to do it quietly, "You better..." I silenced him with a hand over his mouth.

We were all standing, three abreast on the far side of a small outcrop. I mean a small outcrop! Maybe eighteen inches. You can imagine our distress when one individual walked straight toward us, then turned and sat on a rock very nearly in front of me. I could reach out and tap him on the shoulder. I turned to look at Liz, and I could easily see the gleaming whites of her eyes, they were beaming with that look of sheer panic on her face. He just sat smoking a cigarette and relaxing.

Fifteen minutes later, when he hadn't moved, I thought that the time had come to remove him from this existence. I slowly, oh so painfully slowly withdrew the knife my father had given me from its scabbard. I held it up for Liz and Seth to see and I pointed at the visitor on the rock. Again, torturously slowly leaned my M-4 up against the rock wall we were hiding against.

I already knew where and how I was going to cut this clown. I just had to do it. The thought of it made me break out in the coldest sweat. My hands were suddenly clammy. I crouched, left hand raised to cover his mouth, right hand raised holding the knife. I leaned over him. Well, this was it. My luck was up. I decided to make my move... Now! I heard somebody call to somebody else

I Lunged! I heard the visitor answer up.

I froze in my downward motions and hung, seemingly in mid-air, precariously balanced on the very tips of toes. My hand just inches from his mouth, the tip of my blade inches from his neck, the breath in my lungs was caught in mid throat, still, seconds later, precariously balanced on my very tip toes. With my head just 6 inches away from his, I listened while the two chatted for about thirty seconds. My heart pounded! The surge of blood coursing through my head, roared with massive each heart beat.

Then, as if he'd suddenly become bored with our company, the visitor stood and left. How he managed to stand without bumping into me will continue to puzzle me to the grave.

Eventually, I stood up straight and sheathed my knife. My heart would not beat again for another month. As the convoy settled in for the night, we just walked across the wadi, banking that they couldn't see us and if they did, could not make out who we were. Then we quietly climbed the gently rising slope of the far bank, and hurriedly put distance between us.

* * * *

02:17
Due to the near complete darkness, we walked by the house a

couple of times as we searched back and forth for it. I had Mugsy in my ear phones, as he watched us pace about through Night Vision Optics. The fact that we could talk to them meant we were probably within a thousand meters. We were only about twenty meters away from the house before we almost stumbled on it. Apparently, the engraver and company were already there because Louie and Mugsy had been there when they showed up at 13:30, in a panel truck parked outside the shack. We took up a position less than a hundred meters away, where we waited for daylight.

I made each of us pull an hour's watch, while the other two napped.

* * * *

05:30
It was still dark, and since Ramadan had passed, nobody was staying up all night eating, anymore. But there was now enough light to see some of the surrounding area and that it had much more vegetation most of Afghanistan. Not a regular Garden of Eden, but all things are relative.

I could feel the familiar tension headache coming on again. Just like when I'm looking down the scope. It must be something about just knowing that combat is imminent. Sucks!

Al Qaeda must be set up like the Red Army of the old Cold War days, in that every Command—Command meaning every single Infantry Rifle Company, every ship, every flight, every squadron, every division or corps had a Political Officer whose responsibility was to ensure that the Commanders actions were within the best interest of the Soviet Socialist Republic. Al Qaeda, apparently had squad Imams, or holy men.

Because shortly after 05:30, one man stepped out of the house and began a relatively quiet call to prayer. Since everybody was inside the house a few yards away, he did not yell loud, but the chant went on for the obligatory twenty minutes. Slowly, two more came out of the house wiping sleep from their eyes. They then made their way to the truck where they retrieved their prayer rugs and positioned them selves to face Mecca. All during the twenty minute call to prayer, the Imam build a small fire and hung a tea pot over the fire on a spit. He then moved to his prayer rug and began his daily prayers.

The problem was, we happened to be way to close in line with Mecca, because I did not see how we could move on these jokers unobserved.

* * * *

05:53
Start Of Action

I rose up from behind my cover and began to move on the shit heads which lay bowing and chanting before me. As I cleared the stand of tall grass in which we had been hiding, I raised my weapon to my should and kept it in the direction of the Imam who was the closest on to me. I timed my exit on one of his downward bows.

I continued to creep quietly and I vaguely heard Liz and Seth raise up and fall in line behind me. The Imam and other two continued to bow and chant for one more round, and still, we had been unseen. Not for long.

The Imam rose up, and saw me. His face took on a stunned expression as we locked eyes for a moment. He reached down to raise the AK which lay on the ground beside his prayer rug. He barely had both hands on it... *Front sight post, up!* Two shots. Squarely in the center of his chest and he fell straight back. Never to move again.

The sound of sudden gun fire certainly roused the other two, I watched as the next one made a mad dash for the open door of the truck. Unfortunately, he got to the door before I could get a sight picture, as he reached into the truck the third shit head came into view from behind the truck, then immediately saw me and ran back to the trucks rear, out of sight. I continued running forward to the trucks door and leaped kicking the door closed on the shit head's legs as he was just trying to exit the cab. The force of my weight against the door, effectively, painfully closing it on his knees, pushed him back inside the cab, flat on his back. I got a glimpse of the AK that he had left in there, as he fell back.

As soon as my feet were back on the earth, the last shit head stepped from behind the truck, back into view, as he raised his AK in my direction. This is a breach of Etiquette that I find most offensive. I flipped the selector switch on my M-4 to full automatic and gave him a burst to his chest for his troubles. Still holding his weapon, he staggered back three half steps and begged for another. So I gave it to him. Remarkably, he was still on his feet so I paid him a long extended burst of fire until he collapsed.

Not forgetting about the shit head a few feet to my left, who I'd last seen a few seconds ago trying to raise his rifle while falling backwards, I turned my attention to him. I was relieved to see Liz had wrestled his AK from his hand by reaching in the passenger side window.

I looked around and didn't see Thurston anywhere, and I was looking at the door to the house when I saw Thurston come out. In his hands he carried his Sig Sauer pistol and he had what a large wooden suitcase. He gave me a thumbs up and a large grin. I guessed that he had gotten what he came for. It was also here when it occurred to me, that he wasn't with the Royal Treasury. Knowing the British hesitation to provide weapons to well trained police officers, it seemed unlikely that they would provide them to mid-level Treasury Bureaucrats, as well. Okay, so Thurston is with MI-5, or perhaps 6. But most likely 5. Who cares?

* * * *

05:54
End Of Action
Two enemy KIA and one enemy prisoner. Not just any prisoner either. This is one who would clearly be aware of the workings of the inner circle of this caper.

I ripped the driver's door open, finally reliving the crushing weight with which I had used against his shins. I couldn't care less about his pain. I reached inside the truck cab, and took him by the front of his shirt and threw him to the ground. He began yammering in Russian and I was grateful that the only survivor happened to be the engraver.

My headache was gone and I actually felt slightly giddy. It's funny how that stress hits everybody differently. Some men just burst out laughing at the surprise of still being alive. Obviously, I get slightly giddy.

I told the Chechnya to shut up and my use of Russian set him back a bit. Because he launched into another filibuster, shortly after a pause to take a breath, my Russian is pretty rusty, but I could clearly make out the words, "Amnesty International." Followed by "ACLU", I turned and took a short hop to launch my boot into his face as though I were taking a free shot at a soccer goal. His head snapped back and to the side and he fell strangely silent. In mid-sentence, too. Go figure.

With both hands covering his face, his body shook with his sobbing and wailing. I slapped his hands away from his face then picked him up again by the front of his shirt. Bringing his face to within a few inches of mine, I snarled at him, "*Stoi!*"

Again, he fell silent. Then I dropped him back on the ground and I muttered under my breath, "*Pisdah!*" Pussy!

Liz came over and cuffed him with some flex cuffs.

Thurston came over to show us the plates. Inside the wooden case were five pairs of plates in various sizes. Trying to impress us and prove that he was the smartest man in Afghanistan, Thurston went on a tutorial.

"You see, we both are in the process of changing our currencies," Thurston said.

"What do you mean? We just changed it over to the new stuff with the fiber strip a few years ago, then we changed the pictures. What now?" Liz asked.

I knew what was coming, so I took all the wind out of his sails, "We're going to print new money in different sizes so that blind people can distinguish between denominations."

Thurston was slightly surprised, "Yes, but your Treasury Department, only just a week ago approved the designs for the new currency. I'm impressed with the workmanship here. We haven't even released the news that we were changing ours. However, here, he was able to carve out plates for the twenty, the fifty and the hundred U.S. dollar bills, and the new fifty and one hundred pound sterling notes. I don't know how they could've gotten the specifications yet."

"What about the paper? Our paper has always been hard to duplicate." Liz chimed in.

"President Obama decided that it would be a tremendous show of trust and further enhance the economy of Pakistan and build even more good will between the west and the Muslim world if we would obtain our paper for the new currency from the Wazirk Paper Company."

"Makes perfect sense to me. I mean if you were really trying to make the U.S. dollar into *Monopoly* money, could you think of a better way?" I asked.

Shaking her head in stunned silence, Liz repeated, "...further enhance the economy of Pakistan.... He wanted to nuke them during the campaign! They were the only people he would consider nuking! The Wazirk Paper Company?"

Thurston, trying to be a diplomat, came to Chairman Obama's defense, and said, "Their web page states that the Wazirk Paper Company has been making the highest quality papers and linens for Central Asian Royalty for centuries."

Now it was my turn to be incredulous, "Really? For centuries? Do you really believe that, Thurston?"

Mister Howell shrugged knowing damned well, that he didn't believe it either.

"Thank you, Thurston. I feel much better about that moronic decision. After all, nobody is going to put bullshit on their web page. I'm sure Chairman Obama came up with this stroke of retarded genius while he was on one of his apology tours, or perhaps while he was golfing. Rendering our currency useless is not on page one of the Saul Alinski playbook, but it is on page two. I would expect no less from an unrepentant Marxist-Socialist.

Liz still not believing everything, "So, you're telling me, that with this paper shipment coming today, and these plates, they would be able to print as much of our brand new currency as they want, and have excellent counterfeits?"

"I've looked at the plates closely for some of our own internal authenticators. Position of bushes, tress, time on the clocks on the art work, and they are all there. The only way they could've done this was if they had copies of the official lithographs. That's the only explanation. The paper wouldn't be close, it would be the same! They could print as much as they had paper, which would apparently be limitless."

I grew tired of the conversation and went to the radio to call this in. Then we dragged the bodies inside the house out of sight. Now we had to wait on the paper.

* * * *

15:30

For no other reason than I didn't care to listen to Tommy Allen's constant complaints about his rash, I sent him along with the plates and evidence, as well as the two civilians, off to meet the extraction bird. As long as those plates were on the ground, there was a chance that they could be recaptured. I felt pretty smug about myself for dumping Tommy.

Just before they left out, the clear distinct sounds of approaching tanks could be hear reverberating throughout the valley, bouncing off of the walls of the surrounding mountains. Great. I'm reminded of the old, Richard Basehard movie, *"Fix Bayonets!,"* "...when you hear the tanks, you know their on to you, kid..." It's funny how the most stupid stuff comes into your mind at the most inappropriate times.

I keyed the toggle switch clipped to my chest, "Hey Mugsy, do you have eyes on those tanks yet?" I asked into the little boom mike on my headset radio. It had a very limited range, only about a thousand meters, we gave Mugsy the satellite radio, and therefore the long distance communications capability and our primary means of communication. Louie had another radio, but only with communication to the Operations Center at FOB Shkin. They would have to forward any traffic to the CJSOTF for us. This was our Alternate Communications plan. We also had contingency and emergency communications plans. The one thing we could not afford to be without was communications. The best intelligence in the world does nobody ANY good, if you can't send it back.

Mugsy came back over the radio, "Not yet, I don't. You'd better get the civilians out of there before the rest of the guests show up." He was right, of course. They'd been hanging around much too long anyways. So, I grabbed Tommy and started shoving them down the path to the Pick up Zone. They could be there in about twenty minutes.

On their way out, Thurston gave me a pat on the shoulder and a shake of the hand, while Liz looked genuinely scared. I told her, "Don't worry. You're going to get out of here just fine. Those tanks are still probably about thirty or forty minutes away." The truth is, Paratroopers are scared to death of Tanks. I have *always* been a paratrooper! It sounded like a hundred tanks, but in reality, when I listened closely with a finely tuned ear, it seemed more like ten, which meant in reality it was probably only five

"I wasn't thinking of me. I'm worried about you." Liz confessed.

"Don't worry about me. I ain't' gettin' planted here. Remember?"

"Yeah. How do you plan to deal with tanks?" she asked.

"I plan to let the two other guys with me deal with them from a distance."

She shook her head in disbelief.

Yeah, I wasn't buying it either.

She gave me a backwards look over her shoulder as she left with Tommy on point and Thurston watching the prisoner. I gave her a slight wave good bye.

* * * *

14:00
I heard the extraction ship at the PZ picking up, Tommy and

company. At the same time I heard that the tanks were twice as loud as they were when my crew left. One could only reasonably assume that they were now twice as close. As if to drive the point home, I heard Mugsy come over my head set, "Hey Rick, I have a visual on that armor now. I'm counting six tanks, so far, about ten Kilometers out."

I pressed the key clipped to my chest, "How do we want to handle it?" I asked.

"Why don't you come up here with Louie and me. We'll formulate a plan. We'll let them have the house. I think they'll have to wait for the paper convoy and the engraver now.

Chapter Ten

Week ending 10/12/09
7 October 2009. 15:30

I watched as the first tank rounded a turn in the road, as it inched its' way towards us from Pakistan. It was an old Russian T-62 medium main battle tank. This is to say that while it is a piece of inferior technology, it is still capable of killing you deader than a brick. Its machine-guns and main gun are all just as lethal as the day they left the factory.

I began a slow steady trot to move against the tanks aggressively. That's the only thing these guys understand. Strength. Aggression. Might. I saw a spot half way between them and myself, about 600 meters away, where there was a low stone wall that ran along side the edge of the road they were on. What the wall was supposed to contain was anybody's guess. These are just common sights that litter the landscape. Why somebody felt the need to build one...who knows?

By the time I reached that stone wall, the tanks, which didn't seem to be moving any faster than I was, were still almost 300 meters away. I lay on the ground along the bottom of the inside wall, parallel to the road. It was our thought that we would just take out the last one in the formation, until there were none. So, I laid in wait for 'Tail gun Charlie', *standard GI term for whoever is last in file.*

I counted as the tanks rolled passed my position, as I felt the earth tremble beneath my chest and hands. I choked on the thick clouds of acrid and nasty ultra-fine dust of Afghanistan that was churned up by the great lumbering armored beasts. Lumbering they were too. Even as a know-nothing Infantryman, I could tell the engines were sounding awful, misfiring, nearly constantly belching thick clouds of black oily smoke, and at least one or two of them I could see visibly lurch forward on it's tracks in spastic bursts of power.

This was no surprise, since it's been decades since the Soviet withdrawal and with no spare parts, no regular maintenance, no specialized mechanical knowledge or training, it's a wonder that these thing even ran at all. But, here they were, rolling passed me at about five or six miles per hour...four...five...six...

* * * *

15:51
Start of Action:
I cautiously rose up and peered over the stone wall looking for number seven. He never arrived. I turned to look at number six, as it rolled further down the road, from north to south, towards the meeting point. All six had somebody sitting up out of the track commander's hatch. This tank in the Red Army of days gone by, used to be manned by a crew of four: 1 Track Commander TC, 2 Driver, 3 Gunner, 4 Loader. If I'd had to bet, and I would have to, I would've bet one, maybe two had a crew of four. Most, probably only had two or three for a crew. I jumped to my feet and leaped over the wall, and took off after number six. I was going to pushes him for the sin of being number six. *PUNISH*

As I took off at a trot after number six and watched the back of the man sitting in the track commander's hatch. I ran up behind the tank and was looking for a hand hold or something to grab on to. I've seen Sergeant Saunders do this a thousand times in combat! I guess it helps to have a welder on the payroll. *Those German tanks must be much more conducive to this sort of combat, than these Russian pieces of shit!* I hopped and threw myself up onto the rear deck of the tank, just about over the engine compartment. *Such a stupid fuckin'g idea!* I knew the engine compartment would be hot, so I angled myself to the left and looked back up at the TC for any sign of awareness. There was none. *How lucky can I be?*

I swung my feet up on to the deck and stood up and drew my Barrette. I had my M-4 slug across my back, but I didn't want the extra loud noise of a rifle shot to alert anybody as to my presence, just yet. I stepped up almost beside the TC then tapped him on the shoulder with the muzzle of my pistol. When he turned to look at me wide eyed, I pulled the trigger and he disappeared down into the hatch. The driver must've heard the shot because he immediately turned to look back for the TC, only to find me bringing my muzzle down towards his face. I pulled the trigger twice and watched his face disappear in a red mire and then I leaped back off of the deck, back over the stone wall, which still ran for almost another hundred meters. Number six, with a dead man at the wheel and another dead man in command, began to veer to its left where it ground to a slow halt.

Our thought was that which ever track had these 'super important Chinese documents' they would stop and go back for the documents when we eventually hit that vehicle. Now, with number six down, they went for almost another hundred meters before they stopped, because I was almost out of stone wall and concealment. The TC from number five, swung his vehicle back toward six, then climbed down from his seat and craw up on to six. I was frantically searching for what needed next. Something to block the road wheels of number five. This would've been much easier to do in Europe with a thousand felled trees and smooth mossy stones everywhere. But here...I looked over my rock selection and I heard the TC for number five call out as he climbed out of the hatch to number six. Obviously he'd just found the two previous occupants dead from clear gunshot wounds. I didn't look, but I could visualize him climbing back into five and trying to describe the scene inside of six to the others over the radio headphones they were all wearing.

Over the rumble of the engines, I could clearly hear the distinctive clank as they all pulled their hatches shut, effectively 'buttoning up'. This was what we'd hope to accomplish. Because now, I had reduced their number by about fifteen percent and reduced their visibility to about twenty-five percent of what it had been a minute ago. After just a few seconds, number five began lurching back towards the road, and assumed the position of 'Tail gun Charlie'. Apparently, the super-duper Chinese documents weren't in number six. As 'Tail gun Charlie' approached my position, I grabbed my rock and crouched on the inside of my wall. When the driver's hatch was just about where I was I jumped over the wall, and placed a nice large round stone at the bottom of the track, between two road wheels of the T-62's Christie suspension system. As soon as I did it, I saw another rock which was perfect for the same thing, I picked it up and did the same thing. The tank could no longer move forward. I grabbed another rock and ran around to the port side of the tank and place one on the track there, between two road wheels, so that now, he could not even turn or pivot steer. He was now, effectively, at my mercy.

I was not feeling merciful.

The other tanks paused for a minute and I took my time, placing both hands on the deck on the port side of the tank, then pushing myself up onto the deck. I stood, drew my Barrette again, and pulled a grenade from the pouch on my web gear. The driver was now desperate to un-fuck himself. He was crashing the hull of the tank forward and backward in an effort to crush the stones that were blocking the road wheels. Eventually, he would accomplish this. My hope was, that he would not accomplish it before the TC grew impatient and curious and opened the hatch.

I knelt on the deck next to the turret, and braced myself with the turret and turret basket, against the constant lurching and shifting of the road wheels against the rock. I left the pin inside the grenade for the time being. Figuring that when the TC finally opened that hatch, I would have enough time to yank it fast before handing it to him.

The driver must've crushed one rock on the starboard side because the tank could now roll an additional foot that it couldn't a moment ago. The other four tanks all stayed there on the road, waiting to see what happened to number five. I cursed the other two bullet sponges for being up in the hills surrounding the action, unable to assist or take part in this cornucopia of armor which lay before them, transfixed and immobile, like a buffet. None-the-less, I continued to ride the Russian stegosaurus like a dime store pony, while I patiently waited with pistol and present. The main gun on the turret began to sweep in a counter clockwise direction. He was looking to see if somebody was approaching on foot. Perhaps he was just about ready to open up. I laid flat on the deck as the main gun swept over me. I didn't want to move with the turret, and thereby expose myself to one of the other tanks waiting up ahead.

He must've felt so comfortable and complacent knowing that there were no Americans around and he was in his backyard and everybody loves the Taliban and...whatever. After a minute, he opened his hatch.

This would be his last mistake.

I heard the TC turn the handle inside the turret. I pulled the pin on the grenade using my ring finger of my hand that was holding my pistol. When I saw the hatch first break open, I let the spoon fly. I now had five seconds and this tank had to be dead. Because there was not going to be a 'take two'. I reached up. When the hatch was three inches open, I fed the grenade into the open mouth. In my mind's eye, I saw the TC looking all bug-eyed at the grenade as it rolled inside, "Oh! What's this?"

I said out loud, "Hold this for a minute, Sir." I then threw myself on top of the hatch, holding it closed so he could not toss the grenade back out. I didn't have the three seconds cook off time, I would've like to have given it, after what seemed like an hour, but was in fact, only five seconds, the detonation could be heard and felt slightly through the hatch beneath my stomach. I stood now atop the latest monument to Taliban Stupidity, forever a fixture on the Afghan countryside. No matter who won, these tanks would probably stay here until the end of time. I watched as the other four tanks now turned tail and took off further down the road to their rendezvous point. It would've been so easy to finish me off in that moment, but they panicked. The deadliest of battlefield sins.

* * * *

16:00
Action Still in Development:

I was out of radio range with Mugsy and Louie, but only for the time it took me to cover 500 meters. They were still maintaining surveillance over the rendezvous point and watched as the four surviving tanks pulled in and set up a rather hap-hazard perimeter.

Now... No. Actually about thirty minutes ago, I was questioning the wisdom of coming on this mission, where there was a very real Armor threat, without brining a single Anti-Tank Rocket with us! I was, in fact, incredulous. Had I spoken to the Brigadier, I would've made certain that he was aware of my objection. Since Mugsy called in that SITREP *Situation Report,* that opportunity didn't arise. At least now he knew we hand our hands full of armor.

"Mugsy, I gotta tell you, I'm still having problems with the logic for not bringing a couple of anti-tank rockets."

He looked at me smiling, "Yes, I thought you might. The reason being that we really didn't want to get bogged down in a major armor engagement, and that our lack of anti-armor resources, would make that a certainty."

Louie looked from Mugsy to me and shook his head, confirming that this made perfect sense.

"You logic is infallible, Mugsy. Now, here I find myself locked in desperate, mortal combat with, not one, not two, not three or four, or for that matter, even five tanks! I now find myself dancing with six flippin' tanks!"

Mugsy was still looking stoic when he said, "Well, this is my most preferred way to deal with tanks, and that is to let somebody else kill them for me. As for your dilemma, well; I'm awfully sorry, old boy, but you should've insisted."

At this, Louie again, took my gaze and nodded his head in agreement.

Had I only known that all I had to do was insist.

"Fortunately for me, I have an idea. Even better still, it requires no help from either of you! You just need to give me your thermite grenades."

"I'd love to, Rick. But you see, those are for our crypto."

"I know what they're for! I also know that there is a more pressing reality that needs to be dealt with, which mean that Operational planning has been overrun by events. Now just give me the flippin' grenades!"

What Mugsy was telling me everybody knew. That when you go on these sorts of operations, all of your communications equipment and all of your Cryptographic Information has to be destroyed in case capture becomes imminent. Usually, this is accomplished by the use of thermite grenades that burn at several thousand degrees, are capable of reducing any vehicle engine to several hundred pounds of scrap steel, or reduce a radio to a pile of melted plastic and circuitry boards, with still plenty of burning power to handle the books containing our codes, frequencies, call signs, etcetera. Each of us carried one.

Now, if I took all three thermites, and capture suddenly became imminent, we should shoot the radios and destroy them that way. I was going to be working like mad with my Bic lighter trying to burn all of the top secret crypto. We're talking about several pads of paper, one of them 2 ½ inches thick and most of the rest, about four books about ½ to ¾ of an inch thick. Such is life.

In the mean time, our Taliban visitors were making preparations to cook dinner. That they would just drive a few hundred meters from where two of them were knocked out by some usseen, evil infidel force, to me, seemed inconceivable. However, here they were. I noticed this about a great many Afghans, in that they don't seem to have a very good frame of reference for time and space.

Now, this perimeter of tanks was within a thousand meters of our firebase at Shkin. The fact that they found nobody at their rendezvous point, didn't seem to upset them, overly. I now theorized that they were going to try to overrun the firebase. With no anti-tank rockets, and no tank killing resources, the light infantry company would be light work for the four tanks. Even with untrained, unprofessional Taliban crew. If I had to guess, it would be for the gas. After all, the whole mess at the Khyber Pass was all about fuel, too. Still, they brought no fuel truck with them, so how they planned to use the fuel was still in question.

* * * *

16:50
Action Suspended
Now, the only reasonable thing to do was wait until dark. I was watching the activities of the remaining four tanks and their crews, which totaled ten, as far as we could see. While Mugsy and Louie were kibitzing *bullshitting or 'chewing the fat'*, I saw one of the Taliban surrounding their rendezvous point bring up from inside one of the tank's holds, an RPG Rocket Launcher *a Russian Anti-Tank weapon RPG=Rocket Propelled Grenade* and a bag of rockets. I couldn't tell how many in the rapidly failing light. But the presence of an RPG brought a ray of sunshine to my gloomy disposition.

* * * *

21:00
Mugsy, Louie and I were dissecting my brilliant plan to deal with these tanks, before actually going forward and doing it.

Mugsy, for the first time, was incredulous, "That's your plan!? Really? To just walk down there, like you own the place and walk up to three tanks and put thermite grenades on the engines? That's your plan?"

"In a nut shell," I said.

Louie chimed in, "I like it. I Love it, in fact. 'Not by Strength. By Guile!' Furthermore, I'm going with him." He stated the motto of the Special Boat Service.

"Don't get me wrong. I love it, too. It's daring. And 'Who Dares, Wins!'" said Mugsy piping in with the Special Air Service motto as well.

"By the way, Louie. You're not going with him; I'm sending you with him. I'll cover the both of you from our new hide. And, bring back a prisoner, too." This was Mugsy's way of taking charge of the mission, thereby removing Louie's *choice* to go with me, thereby making it an *order*. I was a little surprised at just how petty he was being, but not really sure if he wasn't trying to be mildly humorous.

Mugsy repeated, "Who dares, wins."

Louie replied, "Not by strength, by guile."

I had to get my digs in too. "Fuck these Assholes!" Our motto being in Latin, just wouldn't resonate with these two clods.

We all moved bag and baggage to a new hide position that was probably within 600 meters of the little cluster of armor. Mugsy set up his firing position where he could cover the largest field of view. However, the presence of the armor provided plenty of dead space for us to deal with. Mugsy wouldn't be able to engage anybody who was concealed behind a tank or within a field of dead space.

Armed with our thermite grenades, M-4 carbines, and 9mm pistols, we moved off towards their perimeter. Moving with Night Vision on is difficult because your depth perception is a little off. At first, we moved with stealth and caution. When we were within a hundred meters of their perimeter, we just stood up, and walked right in. The light from the moon was fairly bright, but our bet was that nobody would even challenge us. We were right.

Louie walked up to the tank we decided would be his first and climbed on board. He checked the two fuel cans that were lashed to the turret. He left them, and returned to tell me they were empty.

I walked up to my tank and did the same thing, and found one half full and the other empty. I handed the half empty one to Louie and he carried it over to one of the other tanks, where we found both fuel cans were full. We placed the three fuel on the rear deck of the tank, right over the engine compartment. We went to the last tank and found it had no fuel cans.

I told Louie to stand by and give me about twenty or thirty minutes to find that RPG. I had no real idea where it could be. Looking around the perimeter, checking every place where I saw people gathered, sleeping or talking. After ten minutes, I found it by a pair of shitheads that were laid out, sleeping. I picked up the launcher and the bag of rounds. It felt like at least 3 rounds.

I made my way back to Louie and made I contact with him, held up my thermite and gave him thumbs up. With that, Louie visibly pulled the pin on his grenade, and I did likewise. We both turned to our tanks and opened the thin, practically just heavy sheet metal plating that covered the engine compartments to our respective vehicles. Once we were looking at engines, we looked back to each other, nodded, and placed our grenades as near to the center of the engines as possible. Since the vehicles were not really level, it took some balancing.

* * * *

21:52
Action Continued
Once we released the safety levers, or 'spoons', there were a couple of distinct 'pops' as the igniters were struck. To anybody who knew the sound, it would be unmistakable. To the untrained ear, it could be a light bulb busting. The way these grenades burn, like welding torches, from the bottom up, they allow you to hold on to the grenade at the fuse while it's burning, until you have found a nice level surface. Louie and I looked to each other, visibly grinning at the white glow in the engine compartments as our thermites slowly burned their way to earth. This would take a few minutes.

Louie took off to go do the same at the third tank that we had selected, while I covered him. Even as stupid and lazy as these Taliban shitheads were, even they began to take notice. As Louie reached his second tank, he pulled the pin in the same instant that a shit head who was sleeping about ten meters away, suddenly sat up and spoke to him. I was lining up the sights of my Barrette, when he suddenly and violently was slammed back against the earth. A second and a half later, I heard the report of Mugsy's sniper rifle. Louie set the third thermite on its target area and I moved off to the last tank.

I opened the engine compartment and poured the half empty fuel can onto the engine. By now, everybody was awake and moving about the perimeter. One climbed aboard the tank I was at, and looked at me squarely in the face as he started to climb inside the turret. He froze and took the extra second to size me up, during which time, Mugsy launched a round of ammunition that hurled down range and tore into his chest from behind. The impact of the bullet sent him over the other side of the tank as I continued my chores.

I then put one gas can on each side of the engine and fired my pistol into each so that they would be leaking at the bottom of the gas can. I was betting that this was diesel fuel and not regular gas, or maybe even just water. However, the U.S. Army uses plastic for water jugs, so there is never any confusion. While the Taliban are not encumbered by such regulations, it was my hope they would not put water in what used to hold gas. It was diesel, and while diesel burns, it doesn't burn fast or exceptionally hot. What we were trying to do was melt a couple of gaskets, melt some wiring cover, hopefully cause a few shorts, basically ruin the engine. Once the cans were in place, I stepped back a good distance and drew aim with my M-4 carbine and sent a burst of several tracer rounds into the engine compartment. It caught fire. The last tank too, began to glow from the engine. I collected my RPG launcher and rounds and then Louie. We stood by to make sure that nobody tries to remove our grenades or gas cans. Every time, somebody moved, Mugsy put a bullet into the ground in front of their faces. There was still lots of random fire about the perimeter however, while they searched for Louie and I, they fired into any offending shadow.

As the thermites dropped through the bottom of the hull of the tanks, we knew that these tanks would never move again. The only one we weren't sure of was still burning. Louie and I simply slipped out the same way we had come in.

* * * *

22:05
End of Action
Another thirty minutes and we were back in the new hide position. Snickering ourselves silly that we had just pulled it off.

* * * *

24:00
Lights out for Rick. Mugsy and Louie can pull watch over me tonight. *'You should've insisted, old boy'. You fuck! You fuck! You lousy fuck! 'Dreadfully sorry, old boy. You should've insisted'.*

* * * *

06:15
All of the drivers went to their assigned tanks in the morning and attempted to start their engines. No luck. Not a one started. They all went to the engine compartments and began to tinker and toil with them. I knew it was pointless and only about making the appearance of doing everything.

****

06:50
You can imagine my disappointment when, after thirty minutes of tinkering with the engine, the tank roared to life. I watched as the driver climbed out of the driver's hatch and began wiping his hands off. He had a very satisfied smile on his face. I looked him over pretty thoroughly and he could be another Chechnya.

I told Mugsy what I had in mind, then I took the RPG and moved out in the direction of the Firebase. I paused, turned to him and said, "These are the good times."

He looked back at me and said, "Yes they are. Now keep the good time rollin'!"

About twenty minutes later, I was back at the wadi that we'd had to cross the other night. Here, I waited for the tank to come on its approach to Firebase Shkin.

It was still almost an hour before I had them on their 'route of advance'.

****

07:02
I heard the tank begin moving. The unmistakable clank of the treads on the drive and road wheels made my blood run cold. What was worse, I called it right. They were coming for FOB Shkin, and yours truly.

****

07:05
Numerous shots were heard from the location of the rendezvous point. I assumed that Louie and Mugsy were finishing off the remaining armor crew.

Less than a minute later, I heard Mugsy over my headset, "Rick, do you read me?"

"Roger, Mugsy."

"There all taken care of here. You won't be getting anymore surprises from this camp. We'll link up with you in about thirty minutes, if all goes well."

"Roger, Mugsy."

If all goes well. You fuck! You fuck! You lousy fuck!

Say Good Night

* * * *

07:09

I saw the muzzle of the tank's main gun wobbling as loomed over the far bank as the tank made the gradual climb to the wadi. As soon as he crested the bank, he would expose the lightly skinned armor of the hull's underbelly. A piece of cake. If I took that shot. I stood on the opposite bank and took the RPG, loaded and locked a rocket into place, and walked down onto the floor of the wadi.

After a couple of steps, the thin underbelly presented itself so nicely, and I placed the RPG on my shoulder and flipped the safety to fire as I lined up the sight. I didn't pull the trigger for some unknown reason, but stood there instead.

The faces of the Chechnya driver and the shithead in the turret, were a sight that I will take to my grave with glee. The total utter surprise and unmitigated horror, to see me standing there with an anti-tank rocket less than twenty-five meters away. The Chechnya driver slammed on the brakes and threw his hands up in the same instant, surrendering. I hadn't decided whether I was taking prisoners or not yet, but I guess subconsciously, I really already had.

As the tank lurched to it's sudden stop, the shithead in the turret was suddenly slammed, face first into the top of the turret. In that second, I decided to drop the RPG and drew my pistol instead. As the turret shithead pushed himself back up, he saw that his driver was no longer driving so he went to the machine gun mounted at the hatch. A Russian DDSh 12.7 mm relic of the red menace from a bygone era. He grabbed the handles and swung it my way, I fired two shots between his eyes and he crumpled into the hatch.

I lowered my pistol and trained it on the driver. Then I started walking towards him and signaled for him to get out. He complied being quite happy to still be alive. I raised Mugsy on my radio and filled him in.

Once Louie and Mugsy showed up, we set to searching the tank. Louie and Mugsy had already searched the ones we had already taken care of, looking for these critical Chinese documents that were going to bring the world to it's knees. Nothing. Louie carried a sack full of every scrap of paper from inside every tank.

I asked the Chechnya, *"Gdey Kahtiy boomagoo?"*

"Yah neez nihyoo..." He denied any knowledge. I wasn't buying

that shit.

For his lack of knowledge, I smacked him around for awhile but his pleas of ignorance continued. Being a driver, and a mercenary one at that, he may not have been privy to the document's existence. It still felt pretty good to smack him around a little more.

We set up the satellite radio and informed the CJSOTF as to the mission's developments. So there was no confusion of mishaps when we returned to FOB Shkin, I walked back to the FOB about ten minutes in front of the tank, so I could tell the infantry company there not to shoot at the tank or the guys in the funny uniforms. None of us had anything to use for a white flag.

Since I was the only American there, Mugsy and Louie got to ride back. They parked the tank in the middle of the FOB and we took our prisoner to the airstrip to wait for our chopper ride back to Bagram.

Every single officer in the Operations Center at Shkin had to come out and marvel at the tank. Naturally, photos had to be taken of every officer posing on the tank that 'he had just captured'. *'tis the Army way. Bronze Stars for everybody! Everybody in the OPCEN anyways.*

Chapter Eleven

Week ending 10/14/09
14 October 2009, Inbetween the Pakistan border and Jalallabad. 16:10

I crawled up the final slope to one of the hills surrounding Jamaal's adobe 'estates'. Typically called a Qalat, it consisted of an adobe house, surrounded by an eight foot adobe wall. Being a man of substantial power and influence, his property actually had trees and a well. So brazen was the Taliban now that they felt they could live in the open in our area. As though they just went to an office every morning where they filled their clerical duties and returned home to the wife and kids, every night. It was a perfect Afghan house and property, and painted the perfect picture of Afghan domestic tranquility. Fortunately for me, I knew better.

I had wanted to be here about fifteen minutes prior to this time, so I would be on station for Marid's entire meeting with Jamaal. Unfortunately, a stopped vehicle in the road, made me crawl a much wider circuit to get here. Looking down at the compound, I could see that Marid's car was still not present. I lucked out.

* * * *

16:23
Marid's "new" car rolled up in front of the gate to Hacienda Jamaal. Marid had purchased a brand new, 1984 Mercedes Benz, 300D, yellow in color. I hoped he hadn't paid more than $50.00 U.S. for it. I watched as his car rolled to a stop in front of the gate and Marid stepped from the passenger side. Apparently he had acquired a new driver since the last time I saw him. Marid stood still by his car door holding a leather portfolio and he raised his arms while two guards stepped forward. One searched him while the other one covered his partner.

When they were done, one used a radio for a brief second. A few seconds later, I watched as Jamaal walked out of his front door to the small personnel door next to the large main gate. Here, Jamaal opened the door and allowed Marid to enter and escorted him back to his hacienda.

I hadn't seen the guards because I had made my approach from the west, while his front door and main gate face to the south, along a meandering trail that passed for a rode but had no specific name.

Naturally, I had expected some security and if all I had to face was two guards, I'd count myself as lucky. I continued to watch through my binos as Jamaal walked Marid into the house and passed a couple of windows on the west side.

* * * *

16:49
Several lights were turned on inside Jamaal's residence. Through one lighted window, I saw the back of Marid's head and shoulders as he sat on a chair. It was now totally dark with no moon or ambient illumination.

* * * *

16:55
One of the two goons on gate guard walked around the perimeter. I would have to watch for at least another hour to see if they were on any sort of schedule.

* * * *

17:30
Through the west wall windows I saw Marid and Jamaal walk towards the front door. Now, Jamaal walked him to the gate where they made their bows and good byes. I crawled and then walked down the slope to the compound.

* * * *

17:35
Marid and his driver departed from the compound. Within a minute, my Roschand phone vibrated in my pocket violently. This would be Marid, confirming that 'the package' had been delivered.

Since I was only a couple of hundred yards from the walls of the compound, I spoke quietly, "Bali?"

I heard Marid's extremely cheerful voice on the other end, "Is this my friend Mister Binkus?"

"It is. How are you my friend?"

"I'm doing exceptionally well, tonight. I just wanted to call you and tell you that our mutual friend has the property that he has been waiting for."

"This is very good news. Does he have it in the room where you left him?"

"Yes, he does. That is where he conducts all of his business."

"Tell me, does your driver speak English?"

"No, but I told him that we had important investors in America that were waiting to hear the news, so he should not be suspicious at this conversation."

"Excellent. I think that we can find a bonus for you in the budget."

"That would be wonderful. You have a very nice night, Sir."

"You as well, my friend."

Putting the phone back in my pocket, I got to my feet and made a series of brief dashes to the west wall of the compound. Then I crawled along the base of the wall toward the south wall and the main gate, with the two guards stationed there. In the total darkness and with my ghillie suit on, I wasn't worried about being spotted now on the ground.

* * * *

18:05

This time, it was the other guard who made the rounds of the perimeter and he came from the opposite direction. No matter. I was prepared to deal with whatever came. I pressed myself into the very deepest corner of the wall where it meets the earth, making myself as small as possible. I didn't watch him either, so he wouldn't feel my gaze upon him.

I remained absolutely motionless as passed within a step of me and kept walking, as though he had a bus to catch. As he passed, I rose to my feet as quietly as possible, and I took after him, trying to stay as close to in-step with him as possible, to help hide the sound of my foot falls.

After he rounded the corner to the north wall, I trotted the few remaining steps that separated us, then paused. *One thousand, two thousand...* I turned the corner and ran up to his back and leaped! Just like I'd been trained, I captured his throat with my right forearm and brought that fist up toward my face. With my shoulder, firmly behind his head, I pushed it forward as I began to fall to the ground. With my weight now pulling his body down, he collapsed under my arm, with my forearm as a fulcrum; my shoulder pushed his head forward stretching his neck.

There was a brief rustling, as we both hit the ground, then came the sickening wet snap sound from his neck as I broke it. Then came the familiar rush of saliva to my mouth, and within a second, came the gut retching, worse case of dry heaves that I wouldn't wish on anybody. *Fuck! I hate this!*

* * * *

12 October 2009, Bagram
11:00

Brigadier Ferguson was clicking the ball point pen in his hand as her read my report concerning my last contact with Marid. He then stopped clicking and looked at me from beneath his brow, "So, this could be it?"

"Yes Sir, it could be. I'm certainly hoping so."

"Okay, I'm going to make this easy for you," with that he closed the file and handed it back to me saying simply, "Kill him."

"Just like that?" I was incredulous. "Me? You want *me*, to do this...this hit?"

"Yes, why not? It's been yours from the very beginning. He's an illegal enemy combatant on the battlefield. You need no more authority than mine to kill him, so kill him. If it makes you feel any better, I believe you American's have a sayings too. 'Terminate. Terminate with extreme predjudice."

"I'm not killing anybody in cold blood."

He got a rather befuddled expression on his face and said, "So provoke him if you have to. I would've thought you had gotten beyond that years ago. How many times have you done the same thing to somebody in your cross hairs? It's no different."

His logic was inescapable. I still stood there holding the manila folder.

He stood and came around from behind his desk and put an arm around my shoulder. "Look, this is something we've all had to wrestle with at some point. You just have to believe that what you are doing, *really is*...for the greater good. You'll leave for Jalallabad tomorrow."

I squared my shoulders, stood straight and quietly said, "Yes, Sir."

****

9 October 2009, Mehtar Lam
13:15
While at the OPCEN at Mehtar Lam, I checked in the Brigadier to keep him informed of the happenings. He was almost overflowing in his praise for dealing with six tanks, almost single-handedly. When I said his praise was 'overflowing' what I meant to say is that it was acknowledged.

"Yes, six of them now, did you?"

"Yes Sir, six."

"Wehhhlll! Very well done, Rick. Well done, indeed!"

So, I'm Rick again? Indeed! Hmmm... I wonder what's coming down the pike, now.

"Well, this leaves Jamaal with just one card left to play in his hand. This was very well done, Rick. As long as everything is all tied up nicely in a bow, I don't' see why you can't go home upon completion."

Naturally, 'the one card' he was referring to was the earth shattering, world destroying Chinese documents that will allegedly descend upon the earth like a heard of locusts. I was still very skeptical.

"Oh well, get back here to Bagram as soon as you can Rick. Out here."

Rick, again? Hhhmmm...

Wrapping things up, the Brigadier complimented me on my work with the six rather deadly pieces of Russian crap. He also said that since things have been rolling up rather nicely and rapidly, that my return home has been commensurately hastened but I could expect to be home inside of three weeks.

I was immediately suspicious. Especially since this whole matter was still open and unresolved. Why would I already have an exit date?

The Answer: My informant back in July hadn't been lying at all. That they do have people inside the White House and they were asked to apply pressure. When the White House brings its weight to bear, it is considerable. I can hear the dialog now...

"Hi, General Shmucklenutz? Yeah, it's Rahm Emmanuel at the White House."

"Yeah, we did have a good time with that waitress."

"Which bar was that? I think that was the Green Olive in

Georgetown."

"Yeah, it was just like Ted Kennedy and Chris Dodd's time with that other waitress..."

"Yeah, me too. Look the main reason I called was just to see if you got that extra shipment of powdered coffee creamer for your dining facility?"

"Yeah, you did? Good. Yeah the President splurged and got you the Hazelnut flavor. 'Nothing is too good for our troops,' he said."

"It's no problem, General. Say look, there's a Special Forces guy over there now...yeah, a guy by the name of Burns...ahh, no. Yeah, just like it sounds...u-r-n-s...yeah...that's right. Yes, first name Richard... Yes, I suppose that does make his Dick Burns. Yeah, that's funny. Yes, I get it, Dick Burns. Yeah he's been rode pretty hard and put up wet...yeah, the President is really concerned for him. Look, the President and I both want him pulled out of action."

"His unit? He's assigned to the 7th Special Forces now, but he's permanently assigned to the 20th."

"No, I know you're not the Special Operations Command, Commander! But I do know that being the Army Human Resources Command, Commander ought to count for something! Or perhaps we over estimated your capabilities when we appointed you to this post!"

"Yeah, that's right, Shmucklenutz! Unless you want to find yourself armpit deep in camel spiders you'll make this re-assignment!"

"Saint Louis doesn't seem so bad now, does it?"

Oh well, there are worse places to go than home. I knew this because I was currently in one.

* * * *

11 October 2009, Bagram
08:34
"Bali?" I said into my twitching Roschand phone.

"Hello, I'm looking for Colonel Binkus."

I recognized Marid's voice instantly, "Hello Marid. How are you, my friend?"

"I'm doing very well. I am on a very long journey to collect some very important documents."

My interest and curiosity peaked, "Well, how fascinating.

Where are you going to collect such documents?"

"China. It's about a four hour drive to the border, if the roads hold out."

Well, there was absolutely no chance of me going into China to get these. "Well, where and when can I meet you to get a look at these collector's documents?"

"That is the best news of all. I have an appointment to meet with Jamaal and turn the documents over to him at 4:00 p.m., on Wednesday. Perhaps we could arrange a private showing of the documents."

"That would be fine. Can you text me the location of your meeting?"

"Consider it done."

"The very best of luck to you, Marid."

Within five minutes of the call, I received a text message give me the location of Jamaal's home.

* * * *

14 October 2009, In Between the Pakistan border and Jalallabad

18:11

Leaving the dead guard in the dirt behind me, once my stomach settled, I made my way to the northeastern most corner of the compound. Once it was clear around that corner, I began to move on the second guard and made my way down the eastern wall, to the southern corner. I had to move quickly because I didn't want him to miss the other guard before I dealt with him.

Once at the corner, I tried desperately to get my breathing under control. I was convinced that they could hear me heaving a raspy gasp all the way back at Bagram. Once I was at the corner, I listened to the sound of his steps as he shuffled in mindless circles, waiting for his friend to return. I picked up a pebble and cautiously peered around the corner.

He was looking at his feet while he shuffled and I saw the radio clipped to his belt. The next time he was facing away from me, I stepped out from the corner and threw the pebble to the south western corner of the wall, and then I ducked back around the corner. As the noise perked his ears, he turned and started to shuffle towards the corner, with his AK at the ready.

I stepped from behind the wall and cut a wide arch around the front gate, which was now lit as brightly as mid afternoon. I had my knife in my hand and the ghillie suit did little to conceal me as I stood creeping in the bright light. Any vehicle passing on the road would've surely seen me. I had to move quick. I only had a few seconds. The solace came in the knowledge that he would be dead in a few seconds.

As he turned the corner, trying to peer into the darkness, with his eyes used to the flood light illumination, his back seemed as big as a bill-board. I closed the distance between us, with my left hand raised and my knife hand, ready, blade pointed at my target.

When I was within reach, I brought my left hand to cover his lower face and pulled it away from my knife hand, in the same instant, that I stepped back, pulling him off of his feet, I also dragged the blade of the knife across his throat, from left to right.

I felt him struggle against me briefly then I felt his flesh and soft tissue give way to the blade I put there. I felt a splash of hot blood as it shot forth from his throat and coated my right hand and arm.

His body was still bucking and twitching as I dragged it a few more yards into the darkness around the corner. Leaving the front gate, completely empty. I took his bayonet and his AK and rushed to the northern wall of the compound. I wanted to enter compound from that wall, where I couldn't be seen from the road.

Almost tripping over the first guard, I found and took his radio. Then I fixed the other guard's bayonet to his AK and planted it in the dirt at an angle resting the stock against the wall. The bayonet would hold the muzzle in place while I used the stock for a step to get on top of the wall. So, I took a few steps back, got a little momentum, stepped up onto the stock and grabbed the top of the wall, then I swung my legs first to the right, again to get some momentum, then to the left... then onto the top of the wall. Dragging my hips up onto the top, I laid there on the wall.

There was the thinnest sliver of a moon rising which gave me a little illumination. I saw nothing on the ground, so I slipped down and dropped into a crouch. I drew my Berretta and pulled the guard's radio from my pocket. Then I looked at my watch...

18:52; Start of Action

Chapter Twelve

Week ending 10/14/2009
12 October 2009, Bagram

Brigadier Ferguson said, "I don't expect much from these documents, but if they are supposed to be able to rock the foundation of Great Britain. I won't allow it. Not on my watch."

"Don't worry, Sir. I'll have them soon enough.

"Kill him," said Brigadier Ferguson.

"Jamail? Really?"

"Who else?"

"We don't want to flip him, or interrogate him?"

"Kill him. Terminate with extreme prejudice."

* * * *

14 October 2009, In between the Pakistan border and Jalallabad
18:52

I had just left the two men dead in my wake. My stomach was still churning from the dry heaves that came with killing the first one. Funny, I didn't get the heaves after the second. It must've been that sickening wet snap of his neck.

Although the second one was going to haunt me to the grave. As I crept along the west side of Jamaal's house, my mind was stuck on the sensation of that kill. The way that his knees buckled under my weight, the feeling of his head in my hand as I turned his face away from me. The terrible feeling of the blade pressing against and then cutting through skin, tendon, muscle and eventually the cartilage of his windpipe. The sticky hot feel of that splash of blood on my hand and arm. I wiped my hand clean again, at the thought. As his head went slack in my hand and his body suddenly dropped, I heard the air rushing in the windpipe that I had just severed. His body was still flopping about when I climbed the outside wall to get inside the compound.

12 October 2009, Bagram
"Kill him," said Brigadier Ferguson. "Terminate with extreme prejudice."

* * * *

14 October 2009, In between the Pakistan border and Jalallabad
18:52
It's funny the things that go through your mind at times like this; and how fast they move through. As I approached the front of the house inside the compound, Bill Shakespeare was racing through my mind:

> *To be or not to be-that is the question:*
> *Whether 'tis nobler in the mind to suffer*
> *The slings and arrows of outrageous fortune,*
> *Or to take arms against a sea of troubles*
> *And, by opposing, end them. To die, to sleep*
> *No more-and by a sleep to say we end*
> *The heartache and the thousand natural shocks*

I rounded the corner that would bring me to the front door. In just one second, the vice clamped tight to my head. I took the radio that I taken from one of his guards and keyed the mike. I began to make unintelligible noises and guttural sounds, muttering Islamic words every second or two, while at the same time dragging my fingernail over the front of the mike to give it a scratching sound, "...mullah... *scraaatchscratch... ...salamsislamd... scratccchhh,scratchscratchscratch...* Mohamed... Allah... *scratchscratch...*"

I heard Jamaal ask, "Bali?"

"*Muttermuterachacha islachamach mohmedmullaaahh, Allah,*" came my reply through heaving scratching.

"Salemah?"

> *That flesh is heir to-'tis a consummation*
> *Devoutly to be wished. To die, to sleep*
> *To sleep, perchance to dream. Ay, there's the rub,*
> *For in that sleep of death what dreams may come,*

Say Good Night

When we have shuffled off this mortal coil,

I didn't have the heart to tell him that Salemah "hath shuffled off this mortal coil". I stepped up to and off to the side of Jamaal's front door. I tapped at the door with the muzzle of my Berretta. Now it was "*Henry V*" that raced through my mind. I heard the sound of approaching foot steps on the other side of the door...

> *"Once more unto the breach, dear friends, once more;*
> *Or close the wall up with our English dead.*
> *In peace there's nothing so becomes a man*
> *As modest stillness and humility:*
> *But when the blast of war blows in our ears,*
> *Then imitate the action of the tiger..."*

I heard Jamaal open viewing hatch on the door to see who it was, but I stayed out of view and just tapped at the door again with my muzzle. He started yammering as he turned the dead bolt of the lock, as the door eased open, I took then knob and pulled it open before he had even pushed it an inch.

As I pulled the door open, leading with my Berretta, I swung into the door and pressed the muzzle to his forehead and stepped inside the house... *Once more, unto the breach...* As I pushed him into his foyer by the muzzle, his slack jawed expression said it all. I pulled the door closed behind me as I stood there for a very long moment, looking at him from over the top of my sidearm.

"You are Colonel Binkus." He finally muttered. It wasn't a question.

"There's no need to be so formal. You can call me, Binkey."

He looked as confused as he ever had been in his life. I decided to fuel that.

"I have some bad news for you, too. The United States Army doesn't send colonels to deal with petulant little adolescents' like you. The fact of the matter is, I'm just a sergeant. You wouldn't even rate me, except I'm an old drunk, has-been at the absolute ass end of his career. To be honest with you, I find it a little insulting to have to stand here with you now."

"So, kill me." He raised his hands and let them fall to his sides.

"In due course. I was wondering if you'd care to tell me of your Chinese documents."

His eyes betrayed his surprise. "You know about the documents?"

"I do."

His chest swelled up a bit with pride, "Then you know how devastating they are?"

"That remains to be seen."

He took me into his main living room to his desk, where they sat out in the open on top. Uncoiled, like a great might scroll from the Pharaohs. Four large pages, each about 16 x 21 inches and made of linen. He moved toward his desk quickly and I growled at him, "Stop!"

He froze. Still keeping my voice low, I motioned with my muzzle, "step away."

Keeping my weapon trained on him, I stepped behind his desk and pulled the drawers open finding two handguns. A Russian Makarov and a Tokorev. I tossed them on to the desk top, then took the first page of the earth splitting documents. The pages were split in to two wide columns, one in Mandarin and one in English. I held it up beside my view of Jamaal so I could still see him while I read a word or two.

I was finding it difficult to read with only half of my attention on it, since it referenced later paragraphs and stipulations and sub-paragraphs and separate clauses. The gist I was getting here said that Al Qaeda AQ, and its member organizations to be determined and named later, had struck a peace agreement with the People's Republic of China PRC and in so doing would be recognized as a body of people to receive consideration. Also stated in the papers was a promise to provide military aid and logistical support from the PRC to AQ.

"Let me see if I get this," I queried him. "China says they'll provide you with weapons, hardware, and other support in exchange for...what?"

"In exchange for the opportunity to teach their Muslim population in the manner stated in the *Koran* and we will teach them how Islam is at peace with the Communist Party, how we can coexist," Jamaal said, rather proud of himself for his understanding of Communism and his English vocabulary.

Obviously, he'd found some way to get past the Communist Party's absolute Godlessness. "So, you and your people don't have a problem with the Communist Party's no religion requirements?"

"Since the latest raids by our brothers in Russia and martyrs in Chechnya, the Chinese Party has realized that while the party doesn't believe in *Allah*, a very large population in China knows the truth! That *Allah* is all knowing and powerful..."

With boredom, I said, "Yeah, yeah, yeah. Look, I've heard it all before, just shut up now."

"You will see. Once you bring these document's to your White House, once your allies in your coalition know that we have struck a separate peace with the Chinese, that we will receive recognition and assistance, none of your allies will stand with you. None of your Coalition will wish to fight the Chinese to stand with you."

He had a point. He was right about the Coalition allies. Nobody would want to bite off a piece of that fight. I really didn't believe that they had such a deal with the Chinese.

Despite my own strength in my beliefs, there was the nagging doubt... That tiny sliver in my brain which remembered those twenty-five Rucksacks with brand new Chinese issue AK's with a few Mandarin documents. Could they be plants? Something to create enough doubt in my mind... Hell, Everybody's mind, that there really was something to these documents. Even just the one percent chance that they may be legitimate might be enough to reduce the Coalition into, as Abraham Lincoln put it, 'reduce it to a rope of sand'.

I continued to pore over the documents, "What is this Hong Kong clause?"

"The Chinese said that if the British withdraw from the coalition and refrain from any military strikes against us for a period of five years then the Chinese would promise to revisit the issue of another ninety-nine year lease of Hong Kong to England."

"Hong Kong has made a lot of money for the Chinese in the last few years. I don't think they will ever wean their appetite for the Dollar now and Britain's budget has since gotten used to not having to administer that place anymore. I don't think most Britons would think it a prudent trade. Essentially, I'm telling you Jamaal, I am unmoved by your documents. It's all very clever, very interesting. But I believe a tremendous waste." With that said, I pulled the hammer back on my Berretta.

* * * *

12 October 2009, Bagram
"Kill him."

"I'm not killing anyone in cold blood," I protested.

"So, provoke him if you have to. I would've thought you had gotten beyond that years ago. How many times have you done the same thing to somebody in your cross hairs? It's no different."

His logic was inescapable.

* * * *

14 October 2009, In between the Pakistan border and Jalallabad

I thought about 343 New York City Firemen crushed in the World Trade Center that morning. I remembered seeing all those people leaping to their deaths and what layer of hell that must've been in those stairways for that to be better option. I thought about 2000 some Americans murdered in broad daylight on national television and I equated that to a single individual person being murdered 2000 times over and over and over again, on TV. I thought about the New York City Fireman who found a woman's severed hand on the street and when he picked it up he found that it contained the severed hand a small child. I thought about my friend Manu Bajaj, a British Subject working at NASDAQ, who found himself caught on the street when the towers collapsed. Manu, as kind a man as ever walked this earth, who then thought for a very long moment, that he was going to check out. That that beautiful September morning, was doomed to be his last, for committing no greater sin than visiting New York that day. He very nearly choked to death that beautiful day with barely a cloud in the sky, air was of short supply at ground zero, from trying to breathe millions of tons of pulverized cement. He was barely able to make his way to Battery Park where he was evacuated to New Jersey.

Then I remembered the passengers of American Flight 76, who refused *to go quietly into that dark night. Who refused to disappear without a fight. Who raged. Raged! Against the dying of the light.*

"All right. We're through playing," I said. *For in that sleep of death what dreams may come...*

"What?"

"I asked, what dreams may come?"

"Huh?" he suddenly looked confused and pathetic.

In a clear stern voice, I said, "I said, it sucks to be you!" Then, in an instant, I raised my piece and fired. I certainly could've killed him with a single shot, but for whatever reason, I didn't. In that instant that I raised my piece, his expression changed from one of confusion, to one of pride. No doubt proud of his Chinese forgeries. Proud of his anger and hatred to the United States and her allies. Most proud of the death of 3,000 plus of her citizens that day. It was all unfounded and furthermore, it was the perfect illustration as to why pride is one of the seven big ones. The seven deadly sins. My first round struck him in his right shoulder.

We'll discuss vengeance, another of the seven big ones, at a later date.

The look of pride that so quickly turned to confusion in that nanosecond between the time the hammer dropped and the time it took for my bullet to find his shoulder. The expression said, *'There must be some mistake! It's not supposed to happen like this!'*

With my pistol still raised, I fired again, this time striking him in the left shoulder. Apparently, I must've been trying to satisfy a blood lust. My third, fourth, fifth, sixth, seventh and eighth shots all struck him in the torso. Not a fatal wound among them. He staggered backward with the impact of each round, until he found himself against his own wall.

My final shot would be the 'Termination'. All of these shots were the 'Extreme Prejudice'.

Clearly, I had become 'trigger happy'—a phenomenon not uncommon to snipers. I willed myself to stop it. However, he was still alive and I couldn't leave him that way. I walked forward and while his arms were still half flaying, I pressed the muzzle of my piece to the side of his diaphragm just below his left arm pit. With my muzzle point directly at his right arm pit, I looked him in the eye and said, "Say Good Night, Cocksucker," then I pulled the trigger.

In that instant between the time the bullet cleared my muzzle and the time it shredded his miserable heart, I saw in his eyes, again, pride. Pride in what he and his minions had committed on September 11th. A pride that I hope vanquishes him to that 7th circle of hell. Now, I had to deal with my own feelings at this point. Those could be summed up in one word: Shame.

Because I hadn't just shot him dead and then walked out. That I'd been more of a professional and detached myself from the task at hand. It had all been so surreal. As though I were watching something unfold and was not really a part of it. Well, it didn't last long.

I watched as his body fell into a bloody heap on his own floor and I reloaded. Not because I had to, but because I could. Just like all of his cohorts in the quarry, those near the Khyber Pass and all of his tankers at Shkin, I had reduced him from a living breathing person into a mere heap of rags on the battlefield.

I folded the Chinese forgeries and put them into my cargo pocket and walked out the front door. Then I left the compound all together and walked down the road 800 meters to where I had left Tommy.

"Do I need to ask how it went?"

"Nope."

Nothing else was said on the matter.

* * * *

16 October 2009, Bagram
09:10

When I saw the collection of usual suspects in the Brigadier's office, I knew something was up. Moneypenny ushered me into his office to find Liz, and Tommy present, as well as the Brigadier.

"Rick, come on in," he said smiling broadly. Then from his top desk drawer, he retrieved a black leather box, "I wanted to make sure that you got this before you went home."

Moneypenny then read the orders, "By order of her Majesty, Queen Elizabeth and Regina II, of the House of Windsor, the Military Cross is to be bestowed upon Master Sergeant Richard Burns, 7th Special Force Group Airborne, Combined Joint Special Operations Task Force—Afghanistan, Intelligence Operations Section; For your gallantry in action in the face of a vastly numerically superior enemy force on numerous..."

The rest was all a blur as the Brigadier stepped forward and pinned the Military Cross to my uniform jacket. As Moneypenny continued to read the orders the Brigadier produced from behind his desk the citation for the decoration. I had never seen a document quite so elaborate. Whereas the typical American citation is on a standard size 8" x 10" paper, this was perhaps 14" x 20" and the citation several paragraphs long, all surrounded by silver gilding.

I took a brief look down at the medal on my jacket to see the white ribbon with the bold black stripe down the center and the silver gilded cross suspended from the two inch bar at the base of the ribbon. The Brigadier Ferguson handed me the citation and while Moneypenny continued to read, her words were missed as I read over the citation:

"Single-handedly engaged a numerically superior fighting force near the Pakistan border resulting in ten enemy insurgents killed in action...engaged no less than six enemy tanks that were engaged in combat operations against a remote coalition firebase near the Village of Shkin...unhesitatingly braved withering enemy fire on numerous occasions...completed all assigned missions to the utmost of his ability and surpassing the highest expectations..." When I lowered the citation the Brigadier stepped forward, gave me a fine cigar, and shook my hand and took the citation back from me.

Again, conspicuously absent from any discussion was the formation of equipment announcing the arrival of twenty-one new soldiers on the battle field with a completely different agenda than ours. Oh well, not to be mention...

"You should enjoy the moment and we'll get a few pictures. Because when you leave this office, the medal stays here. Your citation is considered classified Most Secret. This means it has to stay under lock and key. However, both the citation and your decoration will be held at the Imperial War Museum and Archives in London, in their classified libraries. So, the next time you're in London, you can come and visit your decoration and citation. However, I'm afraid, beyond these walls, none of it ever happened. You know how it is."

"Yes Sir, I suppose I do. I'm humbled nonetheless. Really. I'm truly flattered beyond words. I had no idea you were aware of most of that stuff."

"What kind of director would I be had I not kept my finger on the pulse of your operations in the field? You know, if you submit a request to our Defense Minister, you can probably get clearance for your wife to come and read it and see it. After, she signs a copy of the 'Official Secrets Act'."

"I'll keep that in mind, Sir. Thank you." *There's no way Kathie is ever going to see this,* I thought to myself. *No matter. Nobody does this form medals.*

Moneypenny was through with her reading and stepped forward and gave me a very long and tight hug. While she was there gently swinging from side to side in my arms, I whispered in her ear, "How are you fixed for batteries?"

She took her face from my shoulder and quietly answered back, "I think I have just enough to get me home. Now you get to put the initials MC after your name." Then she lowered her face and looked me in the eye and gave me a very large bright smile. Then the smile vanished, replaced by a grim look of sadness and she dropped her arms, turned and walked out of the office. I gave her a minute and then made an excuse to go say my good-byes in private.

As I walked down the hall and I passed the coffee room, Moneypenny called out to me, "Rick..."

I acted as though I were on my way to the latrine, then turned and watched her put down her cup and tea bag. She quickly walked to me and wrapped her arms around my neck again. I felt the heavenly softness of those two magnificent swells, pressing against my chest. *Yes! I really am such a pig!* I kept my hands at the small of her back, as she rocked me from side to side. It wasn't until she called me Rick this time that I realized just how infrequently she did it.

"You've been the dearest friend to me. I think because you understood me better than anybody. I'm sure that's because you've been married for so long. You're a little more in tune to the female mind."

"I wouldn't say that! Just ask my wife."

"They told me last night, I'm going home in December. Do stop by and see me your next time in London. Bring your wife." She had this very sly, sinister grin. I nodded but there was no way in hell I would bring Kathie anywhere near her.

"Take care, Moneypenny. It's been great to work with you."

She wiped a tear and I turned, and faded away. Outside, I was lighting the cigar the Brigadier hand given me when the he stepped up beside me and took the light I offered. As he puffed on his cigar and he looked at me from beneath his furrowed brow, "So...have you...given any thought..." He took a deep drag and inhaled it, "to what you'll do in retirement?"

"Actually, I have. I think I'll be a contractor."

"Excellent idea. We're going to start using a lot more contractors, as troops withdraw, never to be replaced."

I simply nodded. I knew things were winding down fast. Everybody knew it too.

As some sort of commiseration speech, the Brigadier offered, "You know, the first time I 'touched the candle,' I left two men dead in my wake." To "touch the candle" is a British term that means to kill somebody, to extinguish their light. This is essentially why I say "good night" before I permanently put somebody's lights out. It's just a thing I've got.

The Brigadier continued, "When we are issued a D-notice, that's what an assassination is, the language reads, 'this individual should be restored to the Queen's Permanent Custody at the soonest possible date'. This is just like your 'extreme prejudice' label."

I simply nodded my head in silence. Then I took a drag on the cigar and asked, "Does it get any easier? To live with it? To do it?"

The Brigadier shrugged, "It depends. Did you have a tough time doing it? Are you having trouble living with it now?"

I shook my head 'no,' to both questions. "It was a little hard to pull the trigger on him, since he was virtually defenseless. I believe it's supposed to be. Well, at least, I want it to be. I think it should be hard to kill somebody that you should have to wrestle with it, to some degree that it should weigh on your soul, at least a little bit. I think that without a certain measure of guilt, I would loose my touch with humanity."

"I didn't think you were going have a problem. Now I'm certain you won't." He grew silent again.

Then a heartfelt pat on the back, "I'll be contacting U.S. Special Operations Command from time to time, to take on...consultants. So if you get your name on the rolls with them, maybe the CIA too, we should expect to be working together again."

"Working with you doesn't get too boring. I'd like that. Again."

"Don't be in any sort of a rush. I do want to go home for awhile, revisit the family, and make sure they're all still home and happy. You understand, of course."

I simply nodded. I was going to do a lot more than just that when I got home.

The Brigadier asked wryly, "So, what sort of *mood* did you leave Moneypenny in this time?"

His stress on the word 'mood' made me wonder if he didn't know absolutely everything. *Surely Moneypenny wouldn't have told him that...?*

"I think she'll be okay. She's a good woman. I'm really surprised she's taking my departure so hard. I've only known her for four months."

"She's probably a little more emotional over your departure that she would care to admit—both to you and herself. I suspect that Moneypenny is not one to make friends easily. No, I believe she doesn't have many friends at all."

I didn't want to get into a lengthy discussion of Moneypenny's psyche, so I let the subject subtlety slide away.

Then Liz came out and shook my hand as well, "I wanted to thank you for guiding me on my little adventure. What's the first thing you're going to do when you land in the states?"

"I'm going to check the terminal to see if the FBI is there to arrest me." Not knowing how much she knew, I wasn't going to give her anything either.

"What happened in Vegas can stay in Vegas. As far as I'm concerned, this looks a lot like Vegas."

My mind wasn't eased. Regardless of what she may think, her colleagues may not agree.

Then I turned to look at Tommy and I gave him a hug and said, "I'm going to miss you most of all Scarecrow!"

A camera was brought in and a few photos snapped. None were forthcoming. That's the way that goes.

On November 6, 2010, I retired from the Army with thirty years of service and began my new career as a "consultant".

About the Author:

After Serving thirty years in the U.S. Army, with twenty-three years in Military Intelligence and Special Forces, the author retired in 2010. He served in the Middle East and two tours in Afghanistan with the Combined Joint Special Operations Task Force—Afghanistan, in support of Operation Enduring Freedom.

Email: Richard_Burns325@yahoo.ca

Also from Damnation Books:

Masked Jihad
by David Bullock

eBook ISBN: 9781615723997
Print ISBN: 9781615724000

Thriller Military
Novel of 104,191 words

An unthinkable plot is hatched and America doesn't see it coming…

Filled with rage against his own country, a man who knows America's weaknesses leads al-Qaeda's next great assault against a nation that, once again, doesn't see it coming. The only chance America has of stopping them is former Green Beret Jake Matthews, now a rookie CIA agent, and his mentor/partner, former SEAL Frank Glawson, who together must unravel the horrifying scheme in time. Their only problem is…they don't have a clue about what's going on either, and even if they did, it may be too late to stop it anyway.

Also from Damnation Books:

Silver's Treason
by Clifford W. Dunbar

eBook ISBN: 9781615724079
Print ISBN: 9781615724086

Science Fiction, Military, Thriller
Novel of 80,000 words

Caught in the crossfire between paramilitaries, drug dealers, rebel guerrillas, and the Colombian Army, US Army Private Jeff Thompson and Silver, his K9 companion, are forced to make their way through the jungles of southwestern Colombia to rescue a drug lord's daughter held captive by rebel guerrillas. Silver, the product of a decades-old breeding project overseen by the American military, possesses supernatural abilities that are barely under her control. When Jeff is surprised by a payoff from the drug lord and seduced by his beautiful daughter, the U.S. Army believes he has gone over to the other side and sends a Retrieval Team after him, with a powerful dog of its own.

Visit us online at:

http/www.damnationbooks.com
https://plus.google.com/115524941844122973800
http://damnationbooks.wordpress.com/
http://twitter.com/#!/DamnationBooks
http://groups.yahoo.com/group/DamnationBooks/
https://www.facebook.com/pages/Damnation-Books/80339241586